Unauthorized Voices

POETS ON POETRY

Annie Finch and Marilyn Hacker, General Editors
Donald Hall, Founding Editor

New titles

Meena Alexander, *Poetics of Dislocation*
Kazim Ali, *Orange Alert*
Martín Espada, *The Lover of a Subversive Is Also a Subversive*
Sandra M. Gilbert, *On Burning Ground: Thirty Years of Thinking About Poetry*
Marilyn Hacker, *Unauthorized Voices*
Grace Schulman, *First Loves and Other Adventures*
Reginald Shepherd, *Orpheus in the Bronx*
Reginald Shepherd, *A Martian Muse: Further Essays on Identity, Politics, and the Freedom of Poetry*

Recently published

Elizabeth Alexander, *Power and Possibility*
Alfred Corn, *Atlas*
Ed Dorn, *Ed Dorn Live*
Annie Finch, *The Body of Poetry*

Also available, collections by

A. R. Ammons, John Ashbery, Robert Bly, Philip Booth,
Marianne Boruch, Hayden Carruth, Amy Clampitt, Douglas Crase,
Robert Creeley, Donald Davie, Thomas M. Disch, Tess Gallagher,
Dana Gioia, Linda Gregerson, Allen Grossman, Thom Gunn,
Rachel Hadas, John Haines, Donald Hall, Joy Harjo, Robert Hayden,
Edward Hirsch, Daniel Hoffman, Jonathan Holden, John Hollander,
Paul Hoover, Andrew Hudgins, Laura (Riding) Jackson,
Josephine Jacobsen, Mark Jarman, Galway Kinnell, Kenneth Koch,
John Koethe, Yusef Komunyakaa, Maxine Kumin,
Martin Lammon (editor), Philip Larkin, David Lehman, Philip Levine,
Larry Levis, John Logan, William Logan, William Matthews,
William Meredith, Jane Miller, David Mura, Carol Muske, Alice Notley,
Geoffrey O'Brien, Gregory Orr, Alicia Suskin Ostriker, Ron Padgett,
Marge Piercy, Anne Sexton, Karl Shapiro, Charles Simic,
William Stafford, Anne Stevenson, May Swenson, James Tate,
Richard Tillinghast, C. K. Williams, Alan Williamson, Charles Wright,
James Wright, John Yau, and Stephen Yenser

Marilyn Hacker

Unauthorized Voices

ESSAYS ON POETS AND POETRY, 1987–2009

THE UNIVERSITY OF MICHIGAN PRESS

Ann Arbor

2013   2012   2011   2010   4   3   2   1

A CIP catalog record for this book is available from the British Library.

Library of Congress Cataloging-in-Publication Data

Hacker, Marilyn, 1942-
    Unauthorized voices : essays on poets and poetry, 1987–2009 /
Marilyn Hacker.
        p.   cm. — (Poets and poetry)
    ISBN 978-0-472-07115-9 (cloth : alk. paper) — ISBN 978-0-472-
05115-1 (pbk. : alk. paper)
    1. Poetry—History and criticism.   2. Poetics.   I. Title.
PN1016.H33   2010
809.1—dc22   2010030237

Acknowledgments

Grateful acknowledgment is given to the editors of the publications in which these essays have appeared, sometimes under other titles. Many of them have been revised for this publication.

Grand Street: "The Trees Win Every Time: Reading Julia Randall"; "Unauthorized Voices—U.A. Fanthorpe & Elma Mitchell"

The Nation: "Mortal Moralities" on Josephine Jacobsen; "Eloquent Ingloriousness" on Tony Harrison; "Provoking Engagement" on June Jordan; "Tectonic Shifts" on Alicia Ostriker

The Women's Review of Books: "Faith and Works" on Marilyn Nelson

Crossroads: Journal of the Poetry Society of America: "What's American About American Form? Phillis Wheatley and the Rest of Us"

Virginia Quarterly Review: "The Mimesis of Thought: On Adrienne Rich's Poetry"

FIELD: "The Young Insurgent's Commonplace-Book"

Poetry London: "Marie Ponsot: Knowledge as a Source of Joy"; "Hayden Carruth, American Anarchist"; "Rediscovering Elizabeth Bishop"

American Poet, journal of the Academy of American Poets: "Three American Women Poets in the First Century of World Wars"

"Deep Travel" was written for the anthology *Deep Travel: Contemporary American Poets Abroad*, edited by Sandra Meek (Ninebark Press).

The essay on the sonnet is an amalgam of one I wrote for *Exaltation of Forms*, edited by Annie Finch and Kathrine Varnes (University of Michigan Press), and a talk given at Somerset House in London, England, under the auspices of the Poetry School.

The essay on Claire Malroux combines elements of prefaces to my published translations of her work: *Edge* (Wake Forest University Press), *A Long-Gone Sun* and *Birds and Bison* (Sheep Meadow Press)—all bilingual editions.

The essay on Vénus Khoury-Ghata combines elements of the prefaces to my published translations of her work: *Alphabets of Sand* (Carcanet Press), and the bilingual collections *Nettles* and *She Says* (Graywolf Press).

The essay on Guy Goffette is a revised version of the preface to *Charlestown Blues*, my translation of his work, published by the University of Chicago Press in a bilingual edition.

The essay on Marie Étienne is a revised version of the preface to *King of a Hundred Horsemen*, published by Farrar, Straus and Giroux in a bilingual edition.

The essay on Emmanuel Moses is a revised version of the preface to *He and I*, published by the Oberlin College Press FIELD Translation Series.

The essay on Hédi Kaddour appeared as the preface to *Treason*, published by Yale University Press in a bilingual edition.

Contents

Deep Travel

I'm sitting at my desk—actually a rather worse for wear pine table—facing the window in my study / bedroom in the rue de Turenne in the third arrondissement. There's a book review I've got to finish by Saturday for *Poetry London* which I've put momentarily aside, but the three books in question are stacked on the table along with a notebook, four earth-mail letters to be answered, an ash tray (mea culpa) and a dozen pages of translations in first or second draft, of a Moroccan Muslim poet and a Jewish poet born in Poland, both of whom write in French. The geraniums in the window box made it through the July heat wave, which seems now like ancient history. It's cool and slightly overcast this afternoon: although the Assumption holiday is not yet past, it feels as if autumn is almost here. Sometimes that means an imminent departure, but not this year, so the thought brings anticipation of friends returning from holidays and the appearance of two French journals I've had a hand in editing rather than any anguish. A Bach flute concerto almost but not quite covers the chuffing of the No. 96 bus as it stops across the street, in front of the café on the corner. At least until I go out to get the evening paper—*Le Monde* hits the newsstands around four—I can pretend there's less disaster in the world than I know there is (I spent an hour this morning signing and forwarding petitions: a cease-fire in Lebanon; five weeks ago it was peace in Gaza, which has still not come about).

Last night, over dinner in the corner bistro with the Lebanese writer Etel Adnan, who lives across the river, and her friend and publisher Simone Fattal, we traded anecdotes about our mutual friend June Jordan, the American poet who died before her time in California in 2002, whose political poems of the 1980s would be all too relevant today. This afternoon, over lunch in another café with the French poet Claire Malroux, we discussed how best to translate the late-sixteenth-century English songs which accompany Dowland's music, a commission for Deutsch Grammophon. Much of life takes place in those semi-public spaces, cafés, restaurants, parks, where, we say to each other, "on va travailler." I often take my own notebook, a book I'm reading (as well as more mundane things like thesis chapters and term papers) in mid-morning to the Sancerre, a café on a busy neighborhood shopping street, but still across the way from a square with vegetation so lush it could be qualified as "wooded," and stay there for the two hours "rental" my espresso has brought me. The waitress usually brings it, with a glass of water, without being asked. Often the combination of being "in public" yet alone, with the tacit agreement of café patrons not to disturb each other, to talk in a low voice, is as conducive to words on paper as is actual solitude. And the attractive nuisance of the computer is absent. (Much of the poem "A Sunday after Easter" was written in the café it describes.)

For twenty years I have lived for part, sometimes most of the year, at the same address in Paris, and returning here feels like returning home. Felt like that almost from the start, which is why I knew I wanted to take the offered lease on the studio apartment of a friend who was moving—and took the first mortgage of my life to buy the studio when the lease was up. Now the studio is a duplex with a spiral staircase, still less than 700 square feet of space. But it's a space that feels like a small house in the midst of a city, in a modest (not to say run-down) building that was likely run-down twenty years after it was built in sixteen-ninety-something, whose winding stairway has been hollowed by centuries of feet. Four windows on the street, with window boxes, and the only view an aperçu of the sets of windows in the building across the street (for Paris, it's a wide street) and the roof, and the sky, changeable, companionable. Always the sky. Last night at midnight, back from walking my friends to the métro, a low full moon sinking below storm-heavy steel wool. Now, pale sunlight behind a diffuse haze of cloud. And it's time to buy the newspaper and consider the world.

What's American about American Form

Phillis Wheatley and the Rest of Us

It is, to me, an obvious remark that all poems are "formal": the writer's decision to arrange a piece of writing on a page with line and stanza breaks which do not correspond to the page's margins creates an implicit and fertile tension, a counterpoint, between the rhythm and pacing of the poem's syntactic structure and that of the visual (and aural, metric) structure created by the poem's typographic setting—a tension which seizes the eye, but can also be heard, often enough, when the poem is read out loud. A line in a poem which ends with the verb "lies," with the following line beginning, say, "beneath the surface," cannot avoid suggesting both meanings of that verb. Alternatively, a poem with a strong accentual meter (whether or not it is one to be found in manuals of prosody) can be "heard" as a poem even if it is printed out as prose, and the interplay between meter and syntax will be perceptible, as W. E. B. DuBois and Hayden Carruth have both proved to readers.

But that's one take on what is "poetry" about "form," or what is "poetry" *tout court,* not what's "American." American poets writing in English, whether they be from the United States or Canada, stand at an intersection of many formal traditions, including the indigenous poetries of Native Americans, the call-and-response forms enslaved Africans brought with them to this continent, which they married to English ballad and hymn forms to create both spirituals and the blues, the continual proximity of Latin American poetry, and, of course, the variegated English language prosodic tradition and its antitheses which came to this continent with the English settlers. That tradition did not remain purely "English" or British for long, as is witnessed by the career of Phillis Wheatley, the brilliant child from Senegal who was writing verse in forms she learned from reading Pope and Gray six years after she was taken from a slave ship in Boston in the early eighteenth century, not speaking a word of English, her age— six or seven—determined by the fact that she was losing her milk teeth. The significance of Wheatley's adoption of English meter can bear much discussion—but so can the fact that the rhythms of Milton's verse and prose informed the cadences of African American religious rhetoric through the early decades of this century, and can be heard echoing in pulpits today. One thing Wheatley's brief and tragic career signally exemplifies is that few American poets stand in the same relationship to the prosodic and other traditions of English verse as even the most politically or artistically radical British writers. All Americans who are not Native Americans / First Nations people are immigrants, or the granddaughters or great-great-grandsons of immigrants, likely to have ancestors who, like Phillis Wheatley or Olaudah Equiano, if under less duress, adopted English out of necessity. Many American poets grew up with the echoes and cadences of another language as background to their English. Just as, at least in New York, the quintessential American foods are pizza and the bagel, and the quintessential American music is jazz, the quintessential American locution is *ein bissel Yiddish y un poco Latino,* and sounds a bit ebonic on the phone. The sonnet on the base of the Statue of Liberty was written by a young Jew of Portuguese descent, Emma Lazarus. It's not surprising that John Berryman had a blackface double, Mr. Bones, in his "Dream Songs," that Elizabeth Bishop wrote a suite of "Songs for a Colored Singer" in honor of Billie Holiday; nor that Gwendolyn Brooks adopted the persona of the white Mississippi housewife whose complaint led to the murder of fourteen-year-old Emmett Till—and gave her the same destructive romantic illusions as the black teenage protagonist of her domestic World War II mock-epic, "The Anniad." As Toni Morrison has pointed out, the constant presence of a racialized Other, sometimes a racial alter ego, is deep-rooted in American writing. But it is, I think, rooted in the American language as well. Along with the metrical/syntactical tension which characterizes any poetry, American poetry is distinguished by another tension, between the *mestizo* American language and the written poetic traditions it inherited more from the English than from any of its other tributaries.

But—and this is an instant "but"—almost every verse form associated with English prosody comes from somewhere else—the sonnet from Italy, the sestina from the *lingua d'oc,* the villanelle from France—even blank verse was introduced in the sixteenth century by Wyatt and Surrey, from an Italian hendecasyllabic model. I'm not sure if any form other than Anglo-Saxon accentual verse is truly indigenous. And this is only congruent with the cheerfully mongrel nature of the English language even preceding its American expatriation, including, as it does, words of Anglo-Saxon, Latin, French, Spanish, Arabic, Greek, German origin, seeming surprisingly ready to integrate, if not embrace, neologisms. We do not have an *Académie anglaise,* still less an *Académie américaine,* to vote on the acceptance of "knish" or "dreadlocks" or "megabyte" into the dictionary. And that is one thing, in a personal parenthesis, which makes the writing of metered and rhymed poetry in English such a pleasure—the juxtaposition of those Latinate, Anglo-Saxon, and other-flavored words, "chickenshit" and "hematocrit," "morose" and "Mykonos," "contextual" and "transsexual," "marathon" and *"maricón,"* "dental floss" and *"meshugass."* That kind of juxtaposition is perhaps most flamboyant when it involves rhyme, but it is also characteristic of American poetry in unrhymed forms and freedoms. Perhaps the American romance with technology, only too briefly chilled by the enormities of Hiroshima and Auschwitz, has made American poets open to acquiring yet another vocabulary, another set of forms: I think of May Swenson's "shaped" poem describing the physics of wave motion, which also describes, without a word extraneous to the stated subject, sexual excitation and release; of physician-poet Rafael Campo's sequence, "Ten Patients And Another," stretched on the grid of two fixed forms: the sonnet, and the patient history every medical student learns painstakingly to take.

American poets seem to have a propensity to invent forms; and our very characteristic contentiousness on the subject, going back to Whitman and Dickinson, is also the sign of an extreme attention. Dickinson's secular transformation of hymnal measures was as deliberate a gesture of prosodic innovation as Whitman's rolling cadences—especially when we remember that Dickinson had Barrett Browning's feminist blank verse epic *Aurora Leigh* virtually by heart. Her decision to avoid the pentameter and privilege a "popular" measure may not have been a consciously defiant one, but was nonetheless momentous for the history of American prosody, and perhaps not unrelated to the subversive appropriation of Gospel cadences by enslaved Africans. While literary modernism in the English language novel has British and Irish sources—Joyce, Woolf, Lawrence, Dorothy Richardson—modernism in poetry had largely American parentage. (Though upon at least one of the frequent occasions when Ezra Pound campaigned for "breaking the back of the iambic pentameter," his next counsel was to "write Sapphics until they come out of your ears"—that is, to learn to hear a metrical music unfamiliar to Americans, or indeed almost any Anglophones.) Marianne Moore, that quintessential modernist, hardly ever wrote a poem which was *not* "formal"—but the forms were always of her own invention, elaborate fixed syllabic stanzas whose metrically irregular lines were visually marked by placement on the page, and often aurally marked by rhymes, with the rhetorical superstructure of the fable. On the subject of modernism, it is important to remember, in a cautionary way, that one of its projects, less laudable in my eyes than "making it new," was to separate poetry from a populist or popular audience, those "women's clubs" Pound scorned, but also factory workers of both sexes, businessmen, farmers, bookkeepers, high school students and their teachers. It's arguable that the lack of critical consideration received by the work of Edna St. Vincent Millay, a decline in "reputation" which began well before her death in 1950, has as much to do with a devaluation of the work of any poet who appealed to a popular audience as with her feminism or use of received forms. In this respect, the work and the aesthetic goals of African American poets from the Harlem Renaissance through the present provide a welcome corrective: their concern seems to have been to bring a linguistically and politically complex poetry to as wide an audience as possible, both within and beyond the black community. *The Crisis* and *Op-*

portunity, where so many of the Harlem Renaissance poets first published, were the journals of the NAACP and the Urban League respectively, and explicitly served a readership broader than a purely "literary" one. Decades later, this poetic "reach" would continue in the work of writers associated with the Civil Rights movement, the Black Arts movement, the anti-war movement, the women's liberation movement.

The American poets of the generation preceding my own who continue to mark my own work were—and are—innovators more interested in how formal transformations illuminate and forefront previously unexamined or marginalized aspects of life and language than in either preserving or revising poetic form for its own sake: I think of Muriel Rukeyser's incorporation of the legal testimony of strip-miners with silicosis, or of the syntax of a refugee child learning English, into poetry, of Hayden Carruth's demotic Vermont and upstate New York dramatic monologues, his Horatian syllabic meditations drawn on the unforgiving northeastern landscape, of Gwendolyn Brooks's Jacobean syntax limning the portrait of an African American community—the south side of Chicago in the aftermath of World War II—with respect, verbal and sensory virtuosity, and ludic irony.

Americans have an indefatigable appetite for self-definition. This is a nation with a contradictory past, a past with very different resonances for its different citizens—the mixed-race African American great-great-grandson of a slave and a man who owned slaves, the Boston Irish bus-driver's daughter applying to Harvard, the Polish Jew whose parents were the sole survivors of their *shtetl*, the Vermont hardscrabble farmer losing the battle against agribusiness and rural gentrification. It is a culture still engaged in inventing itself, so it is no surprise that such invention should also be a tool, if not the central project, of its poetry.

Claire Malroux

Claire Malroux was born in the Albigeois, in southwestern France, before World War II: the war and the Occupation, the death of her Résistant father and the survival of her family are one backdrop to her work. As a child, she left the south for Paris when her father was elected a deputy in the short-lived socialist Popular Front government of 1936. She completed her education at the prestigious École Normale Supérieure. She has remained in the capital for most of her adult life, except for a post-war sojourn in England that led to her engagement with the English language and its poetry (she had studied classical languages and the French canon). Though she was already working as a literary translator, and was the author of two collections of poems, she claims as a signal event in her own literary life her discovery in 1983 of the poetry of Emily Dickinson, which she describes as "an encounter with the uncanny," and the awakening of a "personal affinity." Malroux's ongoing project of translating Dickinson began then, and her own work evolved and developed along with it. She is the author, now, of ten books of poems—four published since 1998.

It was through the poetry of Claire Malroux that I myself first became a translator. A poet since adolescence, an editor and teacher to earn my bread, and a student, reader, and often quotidian speaker of the French language, I had nonetheless never made the leap from hearing the cadences of French poetry and prose in my mind while reading to transposing them into my mother tongue. I had experienced translation only as an adjunct to the process, by responding to French translator friends' and colleagues' questions, exchanges which made me vividly aware of the pitfalls, not to mention the embarrassment of riches, facing any translator of poetry.

I met Claire Malroux at a festival encounter of French and American poets, with Native American poets as the guests of honor, in Grenoble, in late November of 1989. The festival terminated with a midnight Thanksgiving dinner for fifty in the town hall, with the mayor presiding, that may have given the Native American poets several layers of irony to cut into with their turkey.

The festival included readings every afternoon and evening. Many of the American poets present were already working with French translators, and made bilingual presentations. Fewer of the French poets had such alliances, and, since the Americans were, by and large, monoglot, this left the French poets' work outside the space of exchange the festival was meant to facilitate. I had been pressed into service as translator, oral and instantaneous, on several panels, which was probably what led Claire to ask me if I could, in haste, provide a rough translation of a new sequence she intended to read. The on-the-spot translation (done in a pre-Internet hotel room with no dictionaries!), though it served for the reading, was far from true to the poem. But the poem itself, and the process of translation, had engaged me, and, back in Paris, I continued to work on it.

Perhaps if I had been more aware of Claire Malroux's own status as a translator, I would have had less temerity in rushing unprepared into her own text. It was in that same year, 1989, that she received the Prix Maurice-Edgar Coindreau for her collection of Emily Dickinson's poems; six years later she would receive the Grand Prix National de la Traduction for her continuing work with Dickinson, and also for brilliant renderings which introduced contemporary masters like Derek Walcott and C. K. Williams to the French public. But this also meant that the poet whom I was translating (the enterprise soon went beyond one sequence) was the most experienced mentor in the art one could imagine: quite apart from her own bilingualism, she knew as well as anyone what a translation could or could not reflect, in her own poems and others', whether this were a question of rhythm, connotation, or even echoes of other texts which might or might not have resonance for readers in the receptor language. While we have never translated "à deux" in either direction, translation has produced an ongoing dialogue about language, poetic form, lexical connotations, in relation to Claire Malroux's poems and my own, but also to both of our subsequent translations of other poets from and into both languages.

As poets, coming from different traditions, we are very different from one another. Nonetheless, Claire Malroux's work has been subtly inflected by the Anglophone poets she has translated: among others, the Americans Emily Dickinson, Wallace Stevens, and C. K. Williams, the West Indian Derek Walcott, the English Emily Brontë, the Yugoslavian-born Charles Simic, the Canadian/American Elizabeth Bishop, and the Canadian Anne Carson. Her work has developed as well, of course, in dialogue with the French poets she most admires, including Jean Follain, Yves Bonnefoy, and Mallarmé. She is one of those rare poets whose work is informed by day-to-day intimacy with a second language in its greatest variations and subtleties.

Malroux's poems might be said to be, in their own idiom, Dickinsonian, in their heightened, emotive landscapes, their metaphoric shorthand, and their familiar manner with mortality. But they are Dickinsonian often with the "significant absence" of the narrating / lyric "I". A bit of wordplay that only works in English: the "I" in Malroux's poems is more often an "eye," observing, juxtaposing, concluding. The poems are neither autobiographical nor otherwise narrative: something which is not surprising to a French reader, but is more so to someone whose models for poetry are that of contemporary English. A narrative component of some sort is the norm for almost all Anglophone poetry, be it formalist, surrealist, "confessional," post-Beat, rap-inflected, regional, or political. Even Imagist poetry hung on named myths, characters, or landscapes. (There is, of course, the notable exception of the LANGUAGE poets who, not surprisingly, have aroused the interest of French writers and critics.)

Malroux's intersection with the work of Anglophones like Walcott, Bishop, and C. K. Williams may have led to increasing reflection in her own writing upon the action of the agglomeration of events we call "history" on the interweavings of change, memory, and words. Her 1998 *Soleil de jadis* (published in the United States in 2000 by the Sheep Meadow Press with my translation as *A Long-Gone Sun*) examines that interpenetration. *L'histoire* is a triple-barreled word in French, implying at once the macro-pattern of political and economic change, any sequence of events that occurs in fact or fiction (like your grandfather's childhood), and the story that begins "Once upon a time . . ." (*Il y avait une fois*. . .) in the evening on a parent's knee or at a child's bedside. *Soleil de jadis* is a book-length sequence which observes, through a child's eyes, the approach and the devastation of World War II in southwestern France, and the career of her Résistant schoolteacher father, an innovation both in the poet's own work and in contemporary French poetry in general. "History" partakes of all the abovementioned three meanings. The narrative metamorphoses from an incantatory evocation of awakening consciousness in a rural world into gathering fragments of a bildungsroman where family history intersects with self-discovery, fragments that are in turn exploded, dispersed by the arrival of something which seems external and implacable, but is implicated intimately in the protagonist's life: the war, and the German occupation of France that followed.

"I have told this story many times," the poet begins, implying too that it is a story which has been told in many times and places, by different voices, to different audiences. It is one of the quintessential narratives: how a child gains consciousness at the cost of "innocence" when she realizes in precise detail that harm *is* done, that the seemingly eternal moment of childhood is part of the irrevocable passage of history: not "history" in the abstract, but that of the specific time and place in which / of which she becomes aware.

The place here is the Tarn, the southwestern French countryside near Albi, and the time, the 1930s. When the story begins, the poet's father and mother are young elementary school teachers, living, as teachers did in rural France, in an apartment above the schoolhouse which came with the job (since teachers, like soldiers, were assigned to their posts).

My childhood's house is
school and home at once
At night it rises from a corridor of light
cleared by the headlights' beams
when we come back from having left it, Thursdays,
for the city's pleasures

The village school is a stout black building
a stout black governess

. . . .

Once up the stone steps
behind the long white facade striped with vines
coiling around the two arched doorways
(the second one leads to the town hall)
and the two rows of eight windows each
our apartment is to the left on the landing

Augustin Malroux was the son of a miner, atheist and socialist
like his father, married to the daughter of a baker who'd at-
tained some material comfort. He was elected, against the odds,
as a deputy for his district in May 1936, in a climate of social
unrest, strikes, and a desire for change which brought idealistic
and often politically inexperienced members of the Popular
Front into public life all over France. A few months later, the
Spanish Republic began its battle with the fascist Falange, to be
lost in 1939 despite the hopes of a people and of their international allies: an omen of what lay ahead for the rest of Europe.
The Munich Accords between the Third Republic and its allies
and the Third Reich were signed in September 1938. Despite
this perilous compromise, by September 1939, a demoralized,
unprepared France was at war with Nazi Germany, and signed a
humiliating armistice agreement nine months later. France was
divided, with the Germans occupying the northern two-thirds of
the country. (By November 1942, the German army had also
moved into Vichy France—its government, depicted by the poet
from a child's unwittingly ironic point of view, not located in any
capital, but in a spa redolent of shabby gentility.)

Throughout France, there was self-recrimination at the nation's defeat, a desire to place blame that often fell on the progressive movements of the thirties (as well as on Communists,
Jews, and foreigners), accompanied by a rejection of secular,
democratic ideals in favor of hierarchical ones. In July 1940 in
the so-called free zone, only 80 of 649 deputies and senators
refused to vote full powers to the Maréchal Pétain, who favored
active cooperation with the Germans. One of them was the
young former schoolteacher. Swiftly engaged in the Résistance,
he was arrested in 1943 in Paris. He died of dysentery at

Bergen-Belsen in April of 1945, days before the concentration camps' liberation.

We learn, or understand, this as the narrator herself does, a woman remembering through a child's senses what a child perceived. What the child perceives first is her immediate surroundings: the house, and then the village. But this is already a world in which the private and the public mingle: the family apartment is above the classrooms; the little girl's mother, and then her father, are also her teachers; she's aware early on of her father's "ritual and underhanded" ongoing war with the village priest, and of the way her visiting paternal grandfather brings Jean Jaurès's socialist gospel to a few assembled (we can imagine male and middle-aged to elderly) villagers in the town constable's guard-post. Later, she feels her first erotic stirrings toward a young woman pianist, a refugee from the fall of Republican Spain—and we learn almost off-handedly that the president of the Spanish republic-in-exile has taken refuge near by—in a railway-crossing guard's shelter, which recalls the constable's headquarters where her grandfather had spoken, a few years earlier, of Jaurès and equality. We see the child's borders expand: from the house to the whole village—

> The child prepares herself to cross the bridge
> gripping the handle of a basket full of very red cherries
> Far back, at the base of the village
> she took the fork in the main street
> went over the hump in the road which bore
> the house of the director of transportation—
> a Lilliputian bus took the farmers
> to the county seat on market day—

—from her parents and sister to her other grandparents' house and bakery in nearby Albi; from the Midi to the capital, where the young deputy must move with his family; from a tiny fief of which her father is the sometimes-benevolent despot to a vast and baffling world in which he is finally a victim, having freely chosen dangerous actions necessary to his conscience, but nonetheless still a young man, possessed of boyish vanities and ideals.

Claire Malroux's poetry is not, though, a poetry of historical narrative or political engagement. The events that are her story's background, indeed, its backbone, occur almost between the lines. This is primarily a book about memory, how it is inextricably linked to the life of the senses, to objects: the fissured stone of a low wall marking a child's bare thighs on a summer day; the stiff crusted texture of an embroidered cushion; the acrid smell of disinfectant pervading the rudimentary toilets in the school courtyard. All the poet's ideas are indeed embodied in numinous things from which events reverberate:

> I enter that parental bedroom
> whose mortuary wallpaper flowers
> now surround an empty grave
> I'm greeted by the grimace of a child's bust
> perched on a spindly stool
> which, despite its vocation,
> never held a single hat
> In one drawer of the mahogany bureau
> a pair of men's white shorts
> bathe in a smell of mothballs
> folded beside a telescope in its leather case
> Even the word "shorts" is new
> recently added to the dictionary

Even her father's death is here prefigured by the older narrator's finding in a drawer this young man's sportswear, never worn, immaculate as a shroud. As the French poet-critic Alain Borer wrote of this book: "The poem becomes a fabric woven of details (a definition of narrative). But it's the objects, those carriers of story and history, which undertake the telling, or are taken along by it."

This lyric narrative is a bold innovation in contemporary French poetry, largely dominated by work of Mallarméan abstraction and minimalism, by the mandarin wordplay of OuLiPo. Surrealism admitted a poetry inclusive of the quotidian, but it too in general eschewed the long narrative poem which can be "read like a novel"—especially a poem which insists, as does a novel, upon the ways in which the trajectory of an individual's story is inflected by the agglomeration of events called "history." (Exceptions, of course, come to mind: Jacques

Roubaud's chronicle of bereavement and mourning, *Quelque chose noir,* and, more recently, Franck Venaille's 2004 *Hourrah les morts,* re-creating a wartime childhood in the working-class Eleventh Arrondissement.) *Soleil de jadis* was an innovation for Malroux as well, whose lapidary earlier work draws on landscape, seascape, and "inscape," is more aphoristic than narrative, and deftly maneuvers around a first-person singular which it employs minimally and with discretion. Here, too, the protagonist only metamorphoses into an "I" as the book progresses. She is, at the outset, "the child," as if to emphasize that this very specific story has indeed been told many times, in other voices: the story of a child's half-willing and half-resisting plunge into the abyss of history.

Claire Malroux's more recent poems both distance and embrace narrative as the poet examines the texture of memory and of thought. Malroux's poems move between an intense but philosophical and abstract interiority and an acute engagement with the material world. The inevitabilities of time and change, the recuperative but potentially treacherous actions of memory, and the way thought is made concrete through the word are themes central to her work, whatever else is in view. The collections of poems she published between 2001 and 2006 demonstrate an acknowledged cross-fertilization by some themes and obsessions of Anglophone poetry. These include meditations which arise from memories and childhood recollections; the integration of myth with quotidian life; the idea of exile and displacement—as well as her attraction to a longer line and often to a concrete, almost painterly setting which would not have been alien to Elizabeth Bishop.

The garden has been "re-thought" according to new standards
The shacks replaced by uniform tool-sheds
Invasive flowers cut back
An old patch of hollyhocks annihilated
along with other usurping plants
gladiolas dahlias marigolds and sweet william

the Shadow would never have ventured here
but for those who pursue its traveler's dreams
and those of its beloved Baudelaire

the flora has encouraged gold-bellied squash
elegant artichokes perched on high heels
blue-green cabbages the color of eyes and oceans
("The Shadow at Cabourg," *Birds and Bison*)

In Malroux's recent work, often urban in its focus, the strand of
inquiry is elaborated in a contemporary context, while manipu-
lating both metaphor and syntax with a deliberately disconcert-
ing and innovative grace.

The over-sensitive manicurist at the hairdresser's
Was no longer there one day to hold your hand.
Deep depression. Wouldn't she have done better
To use her nerves as salves
On her clients' claws as they purred lazily
Propped in their chairs with a provision
Of fashion magazines stacked on their knees,
And fling her polish in their fresh-stripped faces?
("Facelifts," *Birds and Bison*)

In almost every poem, there is a characteristic and purposefully
unsettling amalgam of past and present that collapses distance
and incarnates through metaphor.

Claire Malroux's most recent published work includes the
poetry collection *La Femme sans paroles* (2006), and also two innovative hybrids. *Chambre avec vue sur l'éternité* (2005) traces the
encounter of two poets—Emily Dickinson and Claire Malroux.
Neither a biography of the former nor a memoir of the latter, it
is a work of the imagination that reenacts the fascination the
American poet has for her French "correspondent," and in
doing so enables a reader to sense the concentration, the disci-
plined lightness, necessary for a poet to immerse herself in, and
then emerge from, such a project of translation.

Traces, sillons, published in 2009, takes the form of a journal
of the poet's process, as she reflects on books newly read,
reread, or remembered, on translating some of those books, on
the changing seasons and interior weathers, and on the emergence of new poems, also given, sometimes in multiple versions,
in the text. A "sillon" is the furrow left by a plow, here, the mental furrows left by tutelary figures like Proust, Rimbaud, Wallace

Stevens, Georges Perec, and, of course, Dickinson. The writer's two residences, Montparnasse and Cabourg—Proust's "Balbec"—are present. So are lively anecdotes about her apprenticeship as a literary translator, in a Paris where literary publishing still proliferated. The book is discreet about companions, family, politics, that which is not writing—but the act of writing is presented with clarity as a confrontation with mortality, the most intimate of relations. The "voice" of the book, while neither "confessional" nor anecdotal, is self-revelatory in a tradition that arcs from Montaigne to Roland Barthes (and includes Auden): the poet marks out, as do those writers, a continuity with the texts she interrogates and praises.

The Young Insurgent's Commonplace-Book

Adrienne Rich's "Snapshots of a Daughter-in-Law"

I wish I could remember when I first read "Snapshots of a Daughter-in-Law." It could have been in 1963, when the eponymous book appeared, but if it had, it would have been a revelation (which I did not have for some years) that other women poets were grappling with the issues I was at twenty, that there might be dialogue and exchange, if not in conversations and letters, in the way a poem in a book calls another poet back to notebook and pen. Like Rich herself at twenty, my literary dialogues on and off the page were largely with men: on one hand, Auden, Lowell, Berryman, on the other, the acolytes of the "San Francisco Renaissance" talking of and reading the work of Jack Spicer and Robert Duncan to their East Coast juniors. I read *Ariel* in 1963, and like other women poets of my generation, I can hear Plathy echoes in poems I wrote subsequently. Rich and Plath (and Anne Sexton) had in common a strong background in and gift for metrical verse and "received forms" upon which they built, elaborated, expanded: in both cases their mature work seems to me much more of an "extension" of this initial achievement than, say, James Wright's abrupt move from metrical toward open forms at roughly the same time. But Rich's work, from at least her third book on, was and is dialogic, a pole away from Plath's insistent interiority. To read a woman poet using and subverting the modernists' collage/quotation/fragmentation techniques—so often employed in mockery of women—in a project of specifically womanly and mordantly feminist inquiry was a heady pleasure. Not to have read this poem at twenty, entered the dialogue then, is a persistent regret, although it was compensated by later discovery.

"Snapshots of a Daughter-in-Law" was Adrienne Rich's first overtly feminist poem. One might say that the earlier "Aunt Jennifer's Tigers" and "Living in Sin" were covertly feminist, but in "Snapshots," Rich not only considered the question of women's aspirations and achievement directly, she placed it within defining social and cultural contexts which would be equally characteristic of her ongoing poetic/political project (though they would grow increasingly less Eurocentric, less focused on the Enlightenment). "Snapshots" is also the first of Rich's equally ongoing series of poetic sequences: nonlinear multipart poems becoming verbal holograms of the subject matter the poet discovered within them as they developed, from "Leaflets" through "Twenty-One Love Poems" to "Contradictions: Tracking Poems" and "An Atlas of the Difficult World," continuing as a central presence in each new collection up through "Tendrils" in *The School Among the Ruins.*

Though "Snapshots of a Daughter-in-Law" marks the young poet's break with the more deliberately groomed metrical verse of her first two books, it is nonetheless informed and, I would say, strengthened by a shadow presence of the sonnet sequence in the shape and structure of many of the sections, in the way many of the strongest lines swell or retract to the pentameter, but also, and especially, by an aptness for nonlinear progression, for intellectual jump-cutting, for building an argument and a narrative with a cinematic accretion of images, personae, and ideas made coherent by the numbered breaks in the poem, rather than a linear or narrative stanzaic progression. The line counts of the ten sections are: 13, 12, 14, 10, 3, 16, 7, 9, 21, 14, many close to sonnet length though none precisely sonnet-shaped. Several demonstrate a distinct volta, the lines following which change direction, sometimes surprisingly, and respond to or comment on the section's opening. Each section is self-contained, and yet each reflects on all the others; the order seems gratuitous but is, rather, inexorable. There are numerous memorable lines, even epigrammatic couplets:

> a woman partly brave and partly good
> who fought with what she partly understood.
> *
> she's long about her coming, who must be
> more merciless to herself than history.

This is a poem, a poet, not afraid of wit, of satire, but the target is most often and surprisingly those with whom the speaker is most identified: *ma semblable, ma soeur.* Nonetheless, its critical reception was virulent enough to discourage the poet from dealing directly with feminist themes, even while her poetry became more immediate in political engagement, for nearly a decade. "A woman feeling the fullness of her powers / at the precise moment when she must not use them" Rich wrote in "I Dream I'm the Death of Orpheus" in 1968.

"It strikes me now as too literary, too dependent on allusion. I hadn't found the courage yet to do without authorities, or even to use the pronoun 'I'—the woman in the poem is always 'she,'" Rich wrote of "Snapshots" in the essay "When We Dead Awaken," some eleven years later. But upon reading the sequence it would be difficult to peg any one of the sections with an autobiographical "I," when indeterminacy—the simultaneous possibility of the "shes" all being one, and of their being different—is part of its power.

> Banging the coffee-pot into the sink
> she hears the angels chiding, and looks out
> past the raked garden to the sloppy sky.
> Only a week since They said: *Have no patience.*

This might be the "nervy, glowering" daughter (not, in fact, a daughter-in-law) of the previous section, yet the description is nearly congruent with:

> Reading while waiting
> for the iron to heat
> writing *My Life had stood—a Loaded Gun—*
> in that Amherst pantry where the jellies boil and scum,

which is, of course, a depiction of Dickinson (encapsulating her line into a narrative pentameter!). There *is* an "I" in the poem:

it is the narrator's voice possessed of and providing all those allusions, angry, disabused, exigent, only hopeful, and not entirely convincingly so, at the conclusion.

The "you," an older woman whose mind is "moldering like wedding-cake" addressed in the opening section, is not the mother-in-law of a daughter-in-law but the mother of an impatient daughter. In many patrilocal cultures, the role of daughter-in-law is, across social classes, difficult and arduous: a young woman leaves her family home to be installed as dogsbody and scapegoat to her husband's extended family, often, in particular, to her mother-in-law, escaped by virtue of having borne and married off a son from the same thankless position: rarely are examples given of mothers-in-law who in empathy refuse to put their daughters-in-law through the trials they themselves suffered. Rich might not (yet) have been thinking of Indian or Indonesian daughters-in-law as she composed the poem (the only "mother-in-law" specifically mentioned is "Nature," from whom, the poem posits, a woman paradoxically stands at far greater remove than "her sons," like Aphrodite in the myth of Eros and Psyche), but the enforced generational or sisterly enmity between (powerless) women is much more focal to the poem than any relationship with men, who are largely present as sources of misogynistic quotations and damning faint praise. The only direct human confrontation in the poem is in the (fourteen-line) third section's second septet—although it is putatively verbal, it is almost erotic:

> Two handsome women gripped in argument
> each proud, acute, subtle, I hear scream
> across the cut glass and majolica
> like Furies cornered from their prey:
> The arguments ad feminam, all the old knives
> that have rusted in my back, I drive into yours
> ma semblable, ma soeur!

—terminating with the transformed last line of Baudelaire's poem "Au Lecteur" from the book he first wished (coincidentally) to call *Lesbiennes*.

"Snapshots" is a commonplace book of quotations and allusions, some in English, some in French or Latin; some complete lines or sentences, some fragmented: Cortot, Baudelaire, Dickinson, Horace, Campion, Mary Wollestonecraft, Diderot, Dr. Johnson, Shakespeare . . . Surely the line "Time's precious chronic invalid" is meant to suggest Alfred de Vigny's "La femme, enfant malade et douze fois impur." The helicopter image in the last stanza is borrowed from Simone de Beauvoir's *Le Deuxième sexe,* and seems to show both Rich and de Beauvoir at a loss to imagine an actual woman freed from the constraints they chronicle.

Rich stated, again in "When We Dead Awaken," that "The poem was jotted in fragments during children's naps, brief hours in a library, or at 3AM after rising with a wakeful child. I despaired of doing any continuous work at this time. Yet I began to feel that my fragments and scraps had a common consciousness and a common theme, one which I would have been unwilling to put on paper at an earlier time because I had been taught that poetry should be 'universal,' which meant of course nonfemale."

Rich's awakening to a feminist (and, eventually, socialist) consciousness has been described by the poet herself in prose and in poems, but here I think she was also describing her discovery of a method of composition which has itself become a leitmotif in many later poems: the joining of "fragments and scraps," whether quotations or described pieces of fabric, bits of pottery dug up on an archaeological site, a yard-sale table spread with salvaged objects—often counterbalanced, as the web of quotations first was here, with an image of speed and distance: the car, the plane, the boat, the helicopter.

It was, when I first discovered this sequence, not only its tentative feminism, but its polyglot, unsparing wit marshalled in the cause of that feminism, even at its outset a difficult and demanding feminism, from a poet and public intellectual who has continued to be "more merciless to herself than history," never abandoning inquiry, erudition, or humor in that scrutiny, that made me remember and keep rereading it. It retains its immediacy and relevance almost fifty years later, as a signal instance of the power of wit in poetry, as a major poet's entry into and instant, germinal subversion of the modernist canon.

The Mimesis of Thought

On Adrienne Rich's Poetry

I have no personal anecdotes about Adrienne Rich worthy of recording. She is a friend I know through her public, published writing, one whom I consider "a friend" because of the importance that writing has had for me over the last thirty-five years, whose presence is a presence in printed words, and therefore never at a great distance. I am in Paris where I live half the time, but where all my books are not. I wanted in particular to reread (but they were absent) *An Atlas of the Difficult World* and *The Dark Fields of the Republic,* an ocean away from a republic whose fields seem particularly lacking in illumination. Instead I started this morning before dawn, in bed, reading poems in the 2002 edition of *The Fact of a Doorframe,* all poems that I have read many times before. This is a body of work that (I know I have written this before) redeems poetry—not that redeeming poetry has ever particularly been Rich's intention. I'm myself a woman of the Left, a feminist, a lesbian, a secular Jew, an American, and a poet, aware how some identities can be chosen or ignored and others constitute facts of one's life immutable as bone structure, and how even this fact can be modified by history. Because I am a poet, the possibilities, the ramifications of what a poet might accomplish—as a writer and as what we now call a "public intellectual," an eloquent representative citizen, have been important to me since I began to read and write myself out of childhood. There were, even in the United States, many examples; some of them were distressing. But Rich was a poet less than a generation my senior who was redefining these possibilities in a way I could understand; in a way that was useful. (It seems clear that one intention of Rich as a poet has been, at least since the sixties, to do something useful, and not only useful to younger poets.)

Rich's body of work establishes, among other things, an intellectual autobiography, which is interesting not as the narrative of one life (which it's not) and still less as intimate divulgence, but as the evolution and revolutions of an exceptional mind, with all its curiosity, outreaching, exasperation and even its errors. (I don't know why, in 1968, she thought Montaigne should "rot in hell". . . . he was, like her, not unfamiliar with intellectuals under house arrest or worse.) Even while Rich was most insistent (and I, her reader, insistent with her) on her particularity as a woman, and an American woman, and on the historical overdetermination of women's experiences and supposed limitations, she was insisting as well, perhaps less intentionally, and the more successfully for that, that a woman's intellectual/political/aesthetic development could provide the emblematic narrative for a generation. Could, like the richly referenced self-examinations of, yes, Montaigne, also provide that emblematic narrative for generations to come. It may be difficult in 2006 to realize how revolutionary such an intellectual stance was thirty years ago. Then, we had in our minds Marguerite Yourcenar writing that women's lives were too secret and too limited to be the subjects of (her own, a woman's) novels, Colette quipping that feminists deserved the harem or the whip; closer to home, the theatrical embarrassment both Millay's work and Rukeyser's provoked in New Critics, and the way any woman poet was praised to the detriment of others. A woman writer, a poet in particular, could unsex herself or attempt to, she could over-sex herself at her peril, she could be the stunning exception or the modest enabler: here, in contrast, was the presumption that the (humbling and humbled, as culpable as triumphant) human narrative was also, was even in primacy, ours. (Montaigne might rate a few years in purgatory for having received a remarkable education devised by his father, then written a brilliant essay on the subject while confining his own daughter's intellectual formation to bigoted, largely unlettered female servants because she was not a son. In this respect, Arnold Rich, Adrienne's father, resembled Montaigne's, and his pedagogy had comparable results.)[1]

Because Rich took a woman's worldview to be emblematic, her inquiries did not stop—as they had not started—at questions of gender. It was with the rage and insights of her feminism that she envisioned, re/vised, to use a word of her creation, Vietnam, World War II, Emily Dickinson, South Africa, Manifest Destiny, the aftermath of the Shoah, and the American Civil Rights movement. The enormous "however" in her work is that it locates each of these investigations in the poet's own physical body as it coexists with her body of knowledge, in her own circumstances and surroundings. It is the link she made youthfully and romantically between "Vietnam and the lovers' bed," which is equally that between the Sudan and an Oakland jazz club, Fallujah and the Brooklyn Public Library, an old man on the roof of a flooded house in New Orleans and the Army recruiter outside Wal-Mart. These juxtapositions, this sense of being, as a poet, necessarily here and elsewhere, elsewhere by virtue of being here, are at the heart of Rich's poetic project. The here / elsewhere / close up / far off alternations have been the propulsion, the form of her intellectual and aesthetic trajectory, the motion of inquiry that enlarges from book to book. Mentioning this may be "Adrienne Rich 101." Yet the poet has become so fixed in some critical or youthful imaginations as a feminist political avatar (to the exclusion of other concerns) while the political changes that she strove and strives for are more and more at risk, and poetry itself becomes both more commodified and marginalized, that it seems worth reiterating. (*Of Woman Born* was translated into French in 1976. Since then, no French publisher has as yet expressed an interest in a book of Rich's *poetry* in translation, although a a skilled translator wished to undertake the project, and the poetic work was included in the important *agrégation* examination in English/ American literature in 1989. I have heard a prominent French male writer/critic dismiss her poetry—with the word "feminist" not uttered but understood—without ever having read it, although he himself translated Whitman, so can presumably read English, and translations in journals and anthologies exist.)

These are some of Rich's poems and sequences to which I have returned dozens of times: "Snapshots of a Daughter-in-Law," "The Demon Lover," "From an Old House in America,"

"North American Time," "Contradictions: Tracking Poems," "Eastern War Time," "An Atlas of the Difficult World," "Calle Vision." There's an older poem called "Translation"—it's not in the selected poems or the Norton Critical Edition on my shelf here—from which I once took an epigraph, which I wanted very much to give to a friend still experiencing that "shared, unnecessary / and political" way of grief last week. There's another poem I don't have at hand, about a Russian poet returning from exile or prison, pruning the surviving geranium and setting her notebook out on the table, which I remember every time I return to the city and work-space I think of as home.

Adrienne Rich expressed in a personal letter in the 1970s the ardent and reasoned wish that I—as a woman and a feminist—would stop writing in metrical forms, a wish I could not fulfill. A poet comes to her work where she finds it and is found by it; I think every kind of poetry possible has its own contradictory social/political history. However, no choice as public as that of poetic form in published work is apolitical. Rich has taught me that, at least. My poetic politics were then a wish to engage in a dialogue with the tradition that formed me as a poet—and to join and affirm the coexistent tradition of women poets using fixed forms in revisionary, adversarial, or indeed revolutionary stances. But I did not have the courage to answer her letter and engage in what might have been another kind of dialogue. I think I have been attempting—by means of poems—to have that dialogue with her since.

Rich herself said in an interview published in *American Poetry Review* in 1991:

> I guess what I'm searching for is a way of staying linked to the past, pulling out of it whatever you can, and continuing to move on. And I'm not sure that a new textual form creates—it certainly *doesn't* create a new consciousness. It can equally be said that a new consciousness, a radically divergent one, doesn't necessarily create a new form either.

It is evident to me as a reader that the carefully conceived formal structures of Rich's own work are an intrinsic part of its memorability, and thus of its pertinence (a poem quickly forgotten by its readers is less than pertinent, however crucial its subject). Her own genius has encompassed the appropriation and radical transformation of poetic form, as well as the integration within poetry of the possibilities of other arts. While it took Rich some decades to "forgive" the sonnet and acknowledge its radical engagements as close in time and space as Claude McKay, Gwendolyn Brooks, and Muriel Rukeyser, she never closed herself to the possibilities established in the sonnet sequence for the sequential not-exactly-narrative, often meditative poem. "Snapshots of a Daughter-in-Law," the signal poem which marked both the young poet's focused attention to woman (historically and immediately) as subject, and her break with the more deliberately groomed metrical verse of her first two books, is nonetheless empowered by the sonnet-sequence-shadow which informs it. Not, I hasten to write, by reference to the sonnet, but by an aptness for nonlinear progression, for intellectual jump-cutting, for building an argument and a narrative with a cinematic accretion of images and ideas made coherent by the numbered breaks in the poem. This is most obviously true of "Twenty-One Love Poems," because of the stated subject, which relates it to one strand of the history of sonnet sequences, and the ten-to-eighteen-line length of the twenty-one poems. But it also forms and informs the superb "Contradictions: Tracking Poems" from *Your Native Land, Your Life,* in which the nonlinear discursiveness of such a sequence enables the poet to construct out of eros, chronic pain, the Shoah, the massacre at Sabra and Shatila, and the canonical changing of the seasons a coherent, kaleidoscopic whole. And it is taken up later, concise, imagistic, and cleaving to the matrix in "From Corrallitos Under Rolls of Cloud."

While the contemporary poet can, if and when s/he wishes, reclaim some of the territory occupied by fiction (Gwendolyn Brooks, George Szirtes, Marilyn Nelson, even James Merrill), and Auden had opera in mind in many of his sequences, Rich's method of narrative makes metaphoric, mimetic use of the techniques of cinema, an art to which she refers openly in many of her early-middle-period poems ("Pierrot le Fou," "I Dream I'm the Death of Orpheus," "Shooting Scripts"): an accretion of detailed visual description of objects establishing a setting or a character; motion in time and place which seems first random and then significant; the alternation of the extreme close-up and long "tracking" shots (found in the "Contradictions" title); the establishment of a narrative and narrative voice as these elements cohere. One might (I might) take this fertile tension between cinema and the sonnet as emblematic of Rich's work—not an antagonism, but the asymptotic motion toward a synthesis, dialoguing in her own distinctive way with the corpus of American ("USonian" and other) and European poetry while investigating the permeability of narrative and reportage. One of the tropes that strikes me as "cinematic" (in its visual effectiveness, combination of still/motion) recurring like a leitmotif in Rich's poems is that of hands turning over small recuperated objects, and beginning to construct something: black and brown bits of pottery dug up on an archaeological site and saved in a dented can ("Shooting Scripts"); a little toy truck and two dusty but good fuses in a long-unopened drawer ("From an Old House in America"); keys and a glass eye in a compartment of a seventeenth-century wooden chest ("When We Dead Awaken"); a jumble-sale table spread with china saucers, silver shoehorns, a 1930s biscuit tin ("Natural Resources"); bronze feathers glued to wings and smashed green bottle-glass ("Marghanita")—and there are others, all sharing the still-potential energy of recuperation/quilting/collage. There are as many counterbalancing (telescoping) images and evocations of speed and distance, moving across a bleak or deserted landscape in a car, usually alone, or in a plane. (Here / elsewhere / close up / far off.) I think of the films of Godard or Abbas Kiorastami, as well as so many American "road movies" in every register. I think of twenty-two-year-old Muriel Rukeyser driving south in 1936 to interview and write about the miners in Gauley, West Virginia. "There are roads to take when you think of your country." The poem as road movie: Rukeyser was one of the first poets to relate film to poetry and see the resonances and parallels.

"I'm not interested in form poems [*sic*]" a student wrote once again this semester, "these formats are not relevant to the expression of black women"—after we'd spent three weeks reading Gwendolyn Brooks. Looking at Rich's entry in a fairly new anthology, I thought again how inaccurate is the expression "moved to [or toward] free verse"—as if there were two kinds of verse, one "free" and one "formal," or "fixed"; as if the "free" in free verse were the same as the "free" of release from prison, as if Adrienne Rich's poems in open/invented forms were somehow equally akin to those of Susan Howe, Robert Bly, Jack Spicer, and June Jordan. Rich's poems, her sequences especially, are as meticulously constructed as any poem in nonce stanzas by John Donne or Marianne Moore, constructed visually, vocally, dramatically, and prosodically. This is attention she has paid (with a genius for it) since the sixties, all the more so after she expanded on the predominating iambic pentameter of her earliest work. It is the knowing formal alternation, a focus at once fragmented and coherent, that marks the mature poet much more than any preoccupation with meter, or any predictable subject or stance. It is the way these sequences follow and mirror the inquiries of thought, discovering their destinations en route.

It occurs to me that one possible approach to Rich's work would be in the context of modern and contemporary poets who wrote/write long poems in sequences, including H.D., Auden, Rukeyser, Berryman, Brooks, Hayden Carruth, Robert Lowell, Derek Walcott, Alfred Corn, Marilyn Nelson. I note that many of these poets' sequences include or are framed by the political and macro-historical in their foci: H.D.'s World War II *Trilogy*, Auden's "Horae Canonicae," Carruth's "The Sleeping Beauty," Corn's "Autobiographies." The long sequential poem necessitates a wider lens, which opens out from the lyrical or anecdotal, even if it began there. But most of these sequences, like those of Rich, are initially envisioned as large in scope. And for this reader, the multifocused, kaleidoscopic poems from "Snapshots" through "Tendril" in the 2004 collection *The School Among the Ruins* are Rich's most characteristic and powerful work: this large poetry made of small objects placed significantly together and swift concepts in motion; a poetry enacting the mimesis of thought.

NOTE

1. Montaigne did confide the first edition of his work to his "fille d'alliance," the twenty-three-year-old self-educated Marie de Gournay, who in turn sought the aid of the scorned blood-daughter Léonor in transcribing the last marginal emendations to the *Essays* after his death.

Rediscovering Elizabeth Bishop

Edgar Allan Poe and the Juke-Box:
Uncollected Poems, Drafts and Fragments
Edited and Annotated by Alice Quinn
Carcanet Press, 2006

Alice Quinn, the charismatic and sometimes controversial poetry editor of *The New Yorker,* now Executive Director of the Poetry Society of America as well, has proved herself an impeccable and courageous critic and scholar of modern poetry with the appearance of *Edgar Allan Poe and the Juke-Box,* her more-than-annotated edition of the unpublished poems of Elizabeth Bishop.

In the three decades since her death in 1979, the reputation of Elizabeth Bishop as a major American poet has increased in magnitude, even overshadowing that of her friend and coeval Robert Lowell, and eclipsing that of John Berryman, whose work seems now unjustly ignored by critics, students, and general readers. Among the many studies of her work (and her life) must be named David Kalstone's 1989 *Becoming a Poet: Elizabeth Bishop with Marianne Moore and Robert Lowell,* Lorrie Goldensohn's 1992 *Elizabeth Bishop: The Biography of a Poetry,* and Brett Millier's 1993 *Elizabeth Bishop: Life and the Memory of It,* as well as innumerable essays by poet-critics as diverse as Anthony Hecht and Adrienne Rich, a piece for the theater based on Bishop's letters, and a mildly scandalous novel published in Brazil. Some of these books made reference to, even quoted completely, poems which did not appear in the 1980 276-page *The Complete Poems 1927–1979,* leaving readers to wonder if, in fact, the critically fastidious Bishop had been more prolific than her oeuvre in print led them to believe. Two (poignant, erotic) poems rescued by the poet-critic Lloyd Schwartz were published in *The New Yorker* in 1991 in the context of his article "Annals of Poetry: Elizabeth Bishop and Brazil." A dozen other previously unpublished Bishop poems appeared *in The New Yorker* in the course of the 1990s and early in this decade; others surfaced in *American Poetry Review, The New York Review of Books,* and *The London Review of Books,* all, we now know, the fruit of Alice Quinn's ongoing research, with the permission of Bishop's literary executor, the life-partner of her last decade. Readers quoted and copied them; clipped them out; pasted them in notebooks; wondered how they had arrived at the journals and what their eventual disposition might be. Either Elizabeth Bishop was alive in Nova Scotia sending poems to magazines (would that it were true) or there was a body of her work extant and under examination much larger than the published books revealed.

In the meantime, Alice Quinn was reading, annotating, and selecting from the more than 3,500 pages of Bishop's writing extant in the Vassar College Library Department of Special Collections, to which the poet had willed them. From this research she has at last produced a book containing some 200 pages of poems and poem drafts, accompanied by a few prose sketches, facsimile drafts of poems, including seventeen stages of the villanelle "One Art," and a 110 pages of informative and lively editorial annotations, placing the poems chronologically, aesthetically, and, as far as is possible, biographically in Bishop's life. The resulting book is a very good read. It is, in fact, a doubled good read, with the revelation of the poems taking unquestioned precedence, but with a plethora of bio-bibliographical (and historical) details, rich in quotations from the poet's correspondence and that of her critics, friends, and associates in the very discreetly headed, 115-page "Notes: Bibliography; Acknowledgments." Rarely, if ever, have pages presented as scholarly apparatus been of such lively interest. (Vladimir Nabokov's *Pale Fire* is a novel disguised as scholarly apparatus to a poem: it could have been a mischievous guiding spirit of this book.)

Here is a poem which Lloyd Schwartz (in a bit of drama described in a letter to Alice Quinn in the aforesaid notes and bibliography) copied from a notebook of Bishop's in 1974 while he was visiting the poet, then almost sixty-three, in hospital; she had been sent for an X-ray of the broken shoulder that was the cause of her confinement. He kept the poem, unpublished, until Bishop's death and for over twenty years afterwards, hoping it would appear in some official or authorized publication. (The poem was published in *The New Yorker* in 2002.) Schwartz mentions that the poem has been set to music by the American composer John Harbison as part of a Bishop song cycle, "North and South," including four other Bishop poems treating love and/or music, among them another previously unpublished poem cited in Schwartz's 1991 essay. This poem, at least, can be said to have acquired a kind of canonical status even before the appearance of Quinn's edition. But it is itself anything but "canonical," in its positing of erotic and psychological frankness in a deceptively nursery-rhyme simplicity of language and form.

Breakfast Song

My love, my saving grace,
your eyes are awfully blue.
I kiss your funny face,
your coffee-flavored mouth.
Last night I slept with you.
Today I love you so
how can I bear to go
(as soon I must, I know)
to bed with ugly death
in that cold, filthy place,
to sleep there without you,
without the easy breath
and nightlong, limblong warmth
I've grown accustomed to?
—Nobody wants to die;
tell me it is a lie!
But no, I know it's true.
It's just the common case;
there's nothing one can do.
My love, my saving grace,
your eyes are awfully blue
early and instant blue.

This is not the Bishop of "Crusoe in England" or of "Brazil, January 1, 1502." Nor is it the Bishop of "Sestina," so discreet that the reader knows neither the cause of the grandmother's tears nor the sex of the child observing her (not easy in English with its gendered possessive pronouns). This is a poet who, like her beloved Metaphysicals, was struck, like a slap in the face, with the juxtaposition of sexual love and death, but who, unlike them (and their defender, Eliot), had neither the consolation of nor the intellectual struggle with faith and a personal God to figure into the mise-en-scène and the equation.

If all the uncollected poems were in this register, even were they of this accomplishment, there might have been an argument for leaving them unpublished (at least for another few decades) not because the above poem is "confessional" (the lover is not named or even gendered; the probable cause of death not specified either; we hope Rochester's "A Song of a Young Lady: To Her Ancient Lover" was quoted jokingly back across the breakfast table) but because one might posit a poet's, as any other artist's, desire to create a coherent oeuvre. But the poems on offer in this particular juke-box are, in fact, of an astonishing variety; what they demonstrate is not a "side" of Bishop that the poet would have preferred to keep hidden, but rather the processes of a poet remarkably exigent with herself who, however, was not only reluctant to destroy drafts, but apt to resuscitate them a year or ten later for development into the fully achieved poems readers know. One could imagine that, had Bishop lived through her eighth decade, knowing her methods and calendars of composition, many of the poems in this collection would have been brought back into the light, perfected (perhaps by the emendation of only a word or two) and published. There are, in fact, poems in this book in all of Bishop's registers: the demotic, even bluesy dramatic monologue; the wry or fable-like observation of the nonhuman animal/vegetable/mineral; the elaborated memory of a significant event from childhood or young adulthood, recollected in less than tranquility; the crisp, metrical love-or-disillusion poem by a twentieth-century Augustan; the interior scenes which violently undomesticate themselves.

Bishop had originally intended the resonant title poem of this book, *Edgar Allan Poe and the Juke-Box,* to close her second collection, *A Cold Spring* (we learn this from correspondence with her then editor, and from Robert Giroux's conversations with Quinn, all cited in the notes)—a poem she worked on and to which she kept returning until well after the book's publication in 1955. It is a quietly astonishing and resolutely difficult poem, about sex, music, alcohol, poetry itself. It is informed by Bishop's reading and appreciation of Poe, but equally by her reading (in translation) of Baudelaire's 1852 essay on Poe, from which she copied this quotation: "Is it not a cause for astonishment that this simple idea does not flash into everyone's mind: that progress (insofar as there is progress) perfects sorrow to the same extent that it refines pleasure . . ." (*Sorrow* is "la douleur" in the original, which also means *grief* and *pain.*) However, Bishop's text in the front of the book is a poem, whatever ideas and theories it (potently) distills in its "block of honky-tonks":

> As easily as the music falls,
> the nickels fall into the slots,
> the drinks like lonely water-falls
> in night descend the separate throats,
> and the hands fall on one another
> [down] darker darkness under
> tablecloths and all descends,

Sorrow (or grief, or pain) and pleasure are coupled in this poem: "pleasure is *exact,* though meretricious / & knows before exactly what it wants," Bishop wrote in a note toward its composition. The consumption of strong drink is described as at once lonely and communal; so, one feels, is the pursuit of sensual pleasure, here disconnected from love, though not from drink, from music, and—paradoxically, in its "exactness"—from poetry. "Je suis la plaie et le couteau," wrote Baudelaire: wounded by wounding, the source of healing, as well as pleasure, in the source of pain (to be echoed in a "shaped" poem called "The Cut" by Bishop's friend May Swenson).

There is a Baudelairean side to Bishop, perhaps most evident in the poems written (completed or in drafts) before her move to Brazil, not only in their revelation of nature in artifice, or vice versa, the epiphanies they experience in low company (think of "The Prodigal") or their lauding and deploring various states of intoxication, but in the correspondences established between disparate events and emotions. There is a poem draft, late in the book, called "Sammy," an elegy for a pet toucan that died accidentally in 1958, when Bishop unwittingly used a poisonous insecticide to delouse him. She worked intermittently on the poem from the time of the event until 1978, referring to it in letters to Lowell in 1958, to May Swenson in 1968, and to Frank Bidart in 1978, with other references in between. Five pages of notes were in her papers. The last line of the last draft is "I loved you and I caged you" (whose bathos does no justice to the poet). A poem-draft from the late 1930s, untitled, whose first line is "In a cheap hotel," ends "He chains me and berates me— / He chains me to that bed and he berates me." There's already a syntactic and thematic parallel to these lines. But it becomes more evident when one knows that the antecedent of "He" in the "cheap hotel" poem is "Love," a horrid night-clerk out of a Liliana Cavani film. The poet had been reading (mentioned in her notebooks, from the notes again) the grim and baroque account of a woman who chained her son to his bed for a decade to prevent him marrying an "unsuitable" girl. Quinn as editor also conveys poet-critic Elizabeth Spires's view, after an interview in 1979, the year of Bishop's death, that this line also may have referred to the poet's guilt after the suicide of a close male friend whose marriage proposal she refused—who wrote "Go to hell, Elizabeth" on a posthumous postcard. "I loved you and I caged you," resonates beyond a dead bird.

Reading some of these poems, one wonders whose exigency excluded them from a book published during Bishop's lifetime. Most often, it was the poet's—but a reader (with the notes at hand) might question how much a rejection from a magazine editor (who, in the case of "The Soldier and the Slot-Machine," an Audenesque quatrain ballad in the persona of a disillusioned, drunken soldier, astoundingly misread it as "light verse") or the opinion of a trusted critic-friend motivated such exclusion, when a different magazine editor, another friend, might have reacted otherwise. Reading other poems and drafts, especially those for the "Aubade" and "Elegy" for Lota de Macedo Soares, one is aware that, however powerful the draft, Bishop might never have been able to complete the sequence, even as a sober octogenarian. Yet Bishop cited "Elegy" as a book-length poem in progress in a grant application completed two years before her death: it is clear (as possible) that she regarded this as work-in-progress for eventual publication, not on a different level of privacy than her other work.

There is a critical orthodoxy proposed in some circles that posits, almost parallel and apace with the New York theater pieces and Brazilian novels about incidents in Bishop's life, her achievements and failings, that any consideration of her work must exist, New Critical style, apart from that work's origins. But the profound revelations of Alice Quinn's edition of Bishop's uncollected poems are not of the identities of lovers, friends, editors, or mentors, or the recounting of actual incidents referred to in a given poem (there is no information of this sort here which may not be found in the extant critical biographies, journal articles, or published correspondence); they are, rather, about the formal decisions and trains of thought (*un train peut en cacher un autre*) which went into the ongoing, often long-ongoing, composition of Bishop's poetry.

Who wouldn't wish, not at all for prurient reasons, to have access to Auden's work-in-progress, just as most of us still read and reread poems he excised from his oeuvre *after* publication—like "September 1, 1939," which blazed across the Web in 2001? Or to drafts Keats had in notebooks at his early death, or Thomas Hardy at his late demise? We have had access to Pound's editing of "The Waste Land," and neither Eliot's nor Pound's reputation, nor the poem's has suffered for it. Would we want to read Yeats's or H.D.'s scraps from the factory floor? Probably. But in Bishop's case, knowing for example that a magisterial poem like "The Moose" was created in 1972 (when a request was made for a Phi Beta Kappa poem at Harvard!) from notes and drafts made decades earlier, we have the peculiar but rewarding sense of being reader-witnesses to much of what might have been, had Bishop simply lived longer. Not many poets compose as Bishop did, putting drafts aside for years, but with the decided intention of completing them, taking them out and working on them intermittently over long spans of years. Seeing this slow motion work in progress (with the frequent illustration of hand- and typewritten drafts in facsimile, sometimes accompanied by sketches) doesn't illustrate how "a poet" works; it does allow readers entry into *this* poet's fairly unique method, and provides as well (I think) a valuable insight from the point of view of *craft* into the poems Bishop included in her published books.

Are there poems in this book that equal Bishop's masterpieces such as "Brazil, January 1, 1502," "The Moose," and "In the Waiting Room"? I don't think so. Are there poems which *contextualize* the major poems, thematically and formally? Absolutely. It is fascinating to know that Bishop had completed only one villanelle, "Verdigris," in 1950 (included here) before writing "One Art" in 1976, but that she had sketched in prose a nightmare "Villanelle" in the late 1930s, and had always been attracted by the form as a vehicle for the ominous and obsessional. While Bishop observed considerable discretion during her lifetime in the publication of love poems, erotic poems, or even domestic poems ("Shampoo" being the only one in which her shared life with Lota figures), now that "a penny life can tell you all the facts," the powerfully reticent sensuality of the dawn thunderstorm ("It is marvelous to wake up together . . .") and of the crystal rock-roses revelatory of the lover's intimate body ("Vague Poem / Vaguely Love Poem") only affirms that Bishop as a poet was as equal to her own biography as she was to the various geographies she inhabited. These poems are fine and finished, and increase the breadth and heft of the complete work. Others, like the drafts of "Homesickness" in both verse and prose, concerning the poet's mother's youth in Nova Scotia, with the related drafts of Nova Scotia poems, leave the reader at once elated (because what there is is so good, because this glimpse of linked composition in two genres is so revelatory) and regretful that the work never was finished. But the satisfaction well outweighs the regret.

The Trees Win Every Time
Reading Julia Randall

In April 1982 I was at Yaddo. It was unseasonably cold and wet: most days the weather precluded the two-mile walk to Saratoga Springs's three bookshops and the bakery-café whose English-style cream teas would have been my reward for working all morning. I was translating part of the autobiography of a black Brazilian rural worker born in 1910 whose life could not have been more different from mine, except for our both being women and both having the stubborn habit of putting words on paper. I was avoiding poetry as I was avoiding thinking about vacancies, uncertainties, in the city life to which I'd be returning. It snowed past mid-month, a good eight inches. The ten people who gathered in the library for the early, somewhat institutional dinners were increasingly able to predict one another's conversations. Shipboard nerves.

It was in the midst of this cabin fever that I—probably looking for Rich, Roethke, or Rukeyser—fingered *The Puritan Carpenter* by Julia Randall out of the shelves of books by Yaddo alumni that lined the off-season dining room and opened it to "To William Wordsworth from Virginia":

> I think, old bone, the world's not with us much.
> I think it is difficult to see,
> But easy to discuss. Behold the bush.
> His seasons out-maneuver Proteus.
> This year, because of the drought, the barberry
> Is all goldflakes in August, but I'll still say
> To the First Grade next month, "Now it is Fall.
> You see the leaves go bright, and then go small.
> You see October's greatcoat. It is gold.

> It will lie on the earth to keep the seed's foot warm.
> Then, Andrew Obenchain, what happens in June?"
> And Andrew, being mountain-bred, will know
> Catawba runs too deep for the bus to get
> Across the ford—at least it did last May,
> And school was out, and the laundry wouldn't dry.

Much of what I wanted from a poem at that moment was in those opening lines. There was a firm, unabashed connection with the mental nation of poets and poetry, its history, customs, and concerns. There was an equally firm mooring in a present moment, offered and realized (August, Virginia, the barberry bush, a year when there'd been both flood and drought) and an imagined future that fixed the speaker in a profession as well as a habitation, contrasting, in a homely example, things as they should be with things as they are. I was engaged by a speaker who addressed both Wordsworth and farm-bred six-year-olds in her interior dialogue. And I liked the deceptively effortless iambic pentameter that carried its reader from interior monologue to imagined dialogue, from summer to fall, from Wordsworth to the first-graders, hardly calling attention to its own suppleness, rhymes cast off like leaves, lush language.

Was it complacent, all this lushness? It was not. A dialogue with language, with poetry, especially as personified by Wordsworth, does not mean that the poet avoids confronting the prerequisites—and the limitations—of language's magical potential:

> What do they tell the First Grade in Peru,
> I wonder? All the story: God is good,
> He counts the children, and the sparrow's wing.
> God loved William Wordsworth in the sprimg.
> William Wordsworth had enough to eat.
> Wye was his broth, Helvellyn was his meat,
> And English was his cookstove. And where did words
> Come from, Carlyle Rucker? . . .

"William Wordsworth had enough to eat." The line may be followed and embellished by metaphor, but it stands, too, a simple declarativesentence in mid-poem. Just as the speaker addresses the future (next season, another generation) along with the past, her colloquy with plenitude does not erase her consciousness of privation, implied since the opening lines, picked up at the closing:

> . . . But sir, I am tired of living in a lake
> Among the watery weeds and weedy blue
> Shadows of flowers that Hancock never knew . . .
> There is not a god left underneath the sun
> To balk, to ride, to suffer, to obey.
> Here is the unseasonable barberry.
> Here is the black face of a child in need.
> Here is the bloody figure of a man.
> Run, Great Excursioner. Run if you can.

Because of what has come before, "the black face of a child in need" is not a poster image eliciting liberal guilt; it is one more piece of descriptive information about Andrew Obenchain or Carlyle Rucker, who have told what they know about the changing of the seasons. This is a poem whose created world includes Wordsworth and hungry black schoolchildren, and will not minimize its commitment to either.

I had the book in my room by then, had reread that poem and gone on to the others. I mention Yaddo, the cold spring, the library, the year, because I had never heard of Julia Randall before then. And yet I read poetry, poetry criticism, and book reviews constantly; I had just assumed editorship of a literary journal devoted to women writers, had researched to teach a course on twentieth-century American women poets. I was excited by my "discovery" at the same time as I regretted the communications gap or lag that had made it somehow as difficult for this reader and this writer to find each other as it would have been had Randall been published only in Australia.

In fact, *Adam's Dream,* the book that followed *The Puritan Carpenter,* was published in 1969 in New York by Knopf (who would temporarily become "my" publisher in 1976—but Randall's book was out of print by then). And, now that I was looking, I found two of Randall's poems in the groundbreaking women's poetry anthology *No More Masks* (edited by Florence Howe, published by Doubleday-Anchor in 1974). Between Denise Levertov and Jane Cooper, according to birth dates, are the poem I've already discussed and "For a Homecoming," also from *The Puritan Carpenter*. This (it could be a companion piece to Mona Van Duyn's "The Fear of Flying") is spoken, in loose iambic pentameter couplets and triplets, by a woman awaiting her husband's return by air, and affirms, most uncharacteristically (for Randall) albeit ironically, that "Man does, woman is":

> Oh, I know
> I'd be content in a cave, and I know that some
> Incredibly curious germ of evolution
> Lets you conceive a rafter and a beam
> And a plastic tablecloth. A single name
> Is all my woe, whatever was first on the tongue
> In the beginning . . .

But who is, in fact, affirming what? Modern American readers are over-accustomed to assuming that the speaker of a poem is, de facto, "the poet" transforming autobiographical material, unless the poem is entitled "Antinous: The Diaries" (by Adrienne Rich) or "The Talking Back of Miss Valentine Jones" (by June Jordan). As far as I know, from discreet biographical notes, Julia Randall has never married, nor taught in an elementary school. Other poems posit children, celibacy, friendships, violence, travel, but this reader soon learned to take each text on its own terms and merit, not to attempt the scrying of one story from their progression. Randall's dramatic voices are less varied than Randall Jarrell's, Pamela White Hadas's, or Norman Dubie's: there are no carnival performers, Russian nobles, GIs, or twelve-year-olds. Nonetheless, the locus of perception shifts, and fixing it is a reward for the reader, appreciating another facet of the maker's skill. The teacher in colloquy with Wordsworth and rural six-year olds is more fully realized because we are not asked to conflate her with "the poet," however much of the poet's information and conviction have informed her interior speech.

When reading Randall's dramatic monologues (which are not always immediately distinguishable from her lyrics), I am challenged to flesh out the speaker and the speaker's story from the poem's clues: language, diction, choice of metaphor. The speaker of "Falling Asleep in Chapel" (from *The Farewells*) is, I think, a man, a father, possibly a clergyman, meditating alone in church at the dawn of Easter:

> It is morning by the clock. Under the dark
> where the loose hound bays night
> on Dead Man, and the cooped cock
> sleeps staring
> the field-bones crack with spring.
> Palm, plume, blade, and tongue
> swell in the valley's skin; waters awake
> for Christ's sake, fools of light
> rising, come in a night,
> come in a night and gone,
> temple and vine,
> child after child, and man,
> after his swollen stem
> has seeded up the sky,
> man gone. And I
> come to this empty house,
> glad of an iron sun
> falling on sterile stone,
> to listen to what I am.
> . . . .
> The dream dies, and I wake
> Adam, in Christ's name's sake,
> Adam newly begun,
> ribbed with creation. See,
> my knees pray, my lungs move
> mounds of tall air. I stare
> into the iron sun. I warm. I walk
> into the nightfall spring . . .

Another poem in the same volume, "Outliving," is the reflection of a woman near seventy on her mother's death, long past, at a younger age. "A Farewell to History" happens in the wake of a violent lovers' quarrel and separation:

> Broke, bloody, bitter, and bereaved, we departed
> the last stand—you to the station (I suppose)

and I to the Emergency Room, where the intern
snickered as he needled my lip and nose.
What I most resented, I didn't understand
then: you broke my glasses. Dark ones on,
I curse you down the passes, across the wide
apple and cow valley, by the North Fork,
the Maury, Buffalo Creek—all the way to work.

Much more domestic female personae are created in "Recipes"
and "A Dream of Reunion" (both from *Moving in Memory*), two
poems that rise from quotidian language and concerns to wider
speculations, presenting traditionally female preoccupations as
springboards to the metaphysical:

Of course I give my recipes away.
Last night I gave Esterlee
the zucchini casserole, and she'll give it to Jessie,
and so it goes. No keeping a secret. I may revert
to Maryland chicken and angel cake. The fit survive
and the raw materials
don't change much in a lifetime, but they change:
there was no tea at Stonehenge.

I poach the flounder in my mother's dish.
The scholars say my mother was a fish.
The strict constructionists say man
strutted around on two legs of his own
all around Eden. Maybe he did,
sharing his recipe with only God, and his spare rib
with woman.

She found apples
good eating. Naturally she shared.
She discovered blood,
guts, seasonings; how to make stock; how best to grow
salads and sesames; and how to raise
bread. One son discovered how to raise the dead
but he never told.

These monologues are united, despite their disparate voices,
by the sense of place. Most of the poems are very specifically located in Maryland or Virginia, by place-names, by descriptions

of landscape, foliage, and seasonal change, by reference to local history. Other places and times are evoked, but whatever personae Randall creates evoke them from a realized, localized present. Like those of Robert Frost, while Randall's speakers ought not to be confused with the auctorial presence, they are mostly citizens of the same county, neighbors: the landscape itself becomes an agent in the poems. Randall's personae differ too strongly from one another to make of her mid-Atlantic states a *paysage moralisé*, corresponding to or inducing human behavior and attitudes. (The speakers quoted might disagree on everything from foreign policy to breakfast food.) But landscape is more than backdrop to Randall, no more interchangeable than people are, or ideas. The opening poem of *Moving in Memory* states:

> I am Piedmont born and bred
> between far hills and sea,
> great hardwoods overhead,
> and waters gently
> falling down to the Bay.
> ("Middle Age, Middle East")

while, in the same volume, a concert commentator's remark invites the speculation:

> . . . the lake and the mountains will do
> as well as anything. The mere suggestion
> conjures Whiteface and Winnisquam
> and all things Appalachian. Equally well
> it conjures Buttermere and Furness Fell.
> But not Naivasha. It's a bracken hill,
> snowy in season; pine is sentinel. The level
> lake may ship a hero or a gull;
> ("Translation")

Julia Randall is currently the author of four book-length collections: *The Puritan Carpenter* (University of North Carolina Press at Chapel Hill, 1965); *Adam's Dream* (Knopf, New York, 1969); *The Farewells* (Elpenor Press, Chicago, 1981); and, most recently, *Moving in Memory* (Louisiana State University Press, 1987). The assortment of presses may partially explain why I hadn't known of her work earlier. Because most books of poetry disappear from circulation so quickly, it seems barely reasonable to discuss a collection published a dozen years ago, while fiction of that vintage is regularly assigned reading in seminars and secondary schools. A poet's latest book does not erase or supersede previous ones; it stands beside them, ought to bring new readers to them as surely as (say) Toni Morrison's *Beloved* renews interest in—and sales of—*The Bluest Eye;* might do so if they were easily available to be read.

Randall's books lend themselves to a unified discussion because her work is of a piece: it has evolved and changed stylistically, but without rupture, and its concerns remain constant. Some of those concerns have already been discussed or touched upon here: the sense of place, and its influence on lives lived in that place; the nature of memory and the memory of nature; the more than seven types of solitude; the conscient individual's relationship to what she or he defines as God; the sense of the past, of human history (and literature) as it influences, or is severed from, the future. She does not write, by and large, about: romantic thralldom; class, race, ethnic, or gender identity; family relationships; national or international politics; yet her poems are often as illuminating or illuminated on these subjects as are more confrontational texts:

> The Curriculum Committee
> is meeting in the Board Room of the Library
> deciding whether a familiarity
> with Xenophon is essential
> to the educated man.
>
> I usually put
> History on the kitchen floor, against dog tracks,
> boot tracks, sink splashes, and spilled beer.
> The tortured children stare
> up, and remind me of the dead
> no-name of suffering unsuffered
> messy creation. I have had
> my world as in my time: beer in the hotel bed-
> room, publication and promotion.
> I have had property and found it good,
> oiling the knee-hole desk and the upright knees.

I have dressed for faculty teas.
I have taught how the poet felt
in Cumberland, the hills about his head,
flat France a memory, and the unwed
partner of his child
paid off. "The weather was mild
on Sunday, so we walked to Gowbarrow." I walked to Carvin's
   Cove

with the dogs. My cousin Xenophon
broke camp, and marched
out of the parched basin
toward the redeeming sea that smacked of home.
            ("A Meditation in Time of War," *Adam's Dream*)

"*And yes, I think / I will vote for Xenophon,*" the poem concludes:
not a foregone conclusion, in the 1960s, among poets thus conscious of man's inhumanity to man, and woman. But Randall's
worldview is a conservative one, in the word's radical sense:
Xenophon is her cousin, Wordsworth (as elsewhere Emily Dickinson and Virginia Woolf) her correspondent: flawed, yes; limited, perhaps, but vital participants in the human conversation.

From the vantage point of her chosen local habitation, Randall has written of being, as well, a mental inhabitant of Gras-
mere and Amherst. Yeatsian cadences echoed in her earlier
music too. They sounded clear in the title poem of *The Puritan
Carpenter:*

> Come, build a cage for the mind.
> Set it water and meat.
> That else would rage through the night
> With honey and gall to eat,
> And bruise its travelling feet
> On the mountain-tracks of desire.

But, in each succeeding volume, Randall's language and
rhythms become more individual. *The Farewells* is an elegiac
book; *Moving in Memory* is, of the four, the most immediate. With
undiminished linguistic precision and formal elegance, the poet
creates, in this newest collection, deceptively transparent and demotic voices, evoking homely things and familiar landscapes that

become numinous precisely through their ordinariness. I've already cited the collector of recipes; in "Thunder," dogs indoors in a storm lead to an exploration of the nature of trust and of fear: the *timor mortis* that is (perhaps) uniquely human and the *terror mundi* that we share with other creatures. A poem entitled "Video Games" can begin:

> In Claude Lorrain, the trees win every time
> The violent spots of color are a game.

and move from the painter's bright, incidental foreground figures to:

> Sue's ship's in bits and Bill has all the castles.
> But Brother Dragon wings the upper air . . .
> Space-fox! Sue yawns into her coke,
> and Sally's boyfriend, bored, begins to stroke
> Sally, but Bill is dead-set now to win.
> Dad, blasted, ambles toward another gin . . .

then back to "Claude's careless creatures," coming to resolution with the speaker, hitherto absent:

> I exist from the beltway, overviewed by
> Channel 13's copter, where right lane
> must turn right . . .

finding in the "poor three-times cut-over woodlot" where she walks her dogs, the diminished image of the trees that triumphed over the tohu-bohu of events in Claude Lorrain's paintings.

The newer poems extend and develop Randall's synthetic ability. As the first-graders followed Wordsworth and the burning bush, the title poem, "Moving in Memory," goes from a local exasperation:

> Moving within memory, I can count
> Virginia, Maine, Vermont,
> and to a wild extent
> Wyoming. I am sick

of my blasted county: Albert Lacey's truck
ten times a day; beltway; industrial park; high density
housing; and Hartline's oak
sickened, that might have seen
Calvert's lieutenants dickering with red men.

to an argument with (this time) Descartes:

> If you'd been born in Cody, say,
> you'd think, but you'd think differently,
> and if you'd been born
> no place (which is a contradiction
> in terms)—say issued straight
> from the Thinker into thin air—
> what would you think about?

and ends with a paean to language as means to "body out / pure
loveless thought," praising, as it goes, Dylan Thomas, and Keats,
who also cared for trees:

> In words, no doubt, those words
> coaxed from our cradle in some foreign tree. We see
> by leaflight, and we name the leaf
> rock maple, sassafras,
> laurel, or blue-eyed grass.

I have read few contemporary poets whose love and attention
for the natural world so clearly integrated and included the
thinking human creature, and human artifact, especially language, with that world. For Randall, there is no dichotomy between Descartes and dogwood, Channel 13, Claude Lorrain,
and tulip poplar, Maryland chicken and resurrection. Randall's
ideal reader is participating, I believe, in the same conversation,
between nature and namer, between knowledge received and
solace sought, between Wordsworth and Carlyle Rucker; he or
she shares the supposition that origins and effects bear observation, that poetry is both a kind of, and spur to, interior examination, and an ongoing exchange with the past and with the
future. Randall does not propagandize, even for poetry; she
does not manipulate readers' appetites or emotions; neither

does she seem to hold that a structure of words is an object of *vírtu* in its own right, to be revered because we are told it is Art. Her poems please in their verbal beauty and balance, but always, also, incite speculation. They do not plead "Weep!" or exhort "Arise!"; they say, plainly and in all complexity: "Think."

Vénus Khoury-Ghata

Vénus Khoury-Ghata was born in Bcharré, a village in northern Lebanon, also the birthplace of Gibran Khalil Gibran, in December 1937. She has lived in France since 1972. Raised in Beirut, she was not the child of the intelligentsia or the diplomatic world like many literary émigrés; she was born to a Maronite Christian family, one of four children of a bilingual policeman and a housewife she's described as "illiterate in two languages." It was the poet's younger brother who first aspired to a literary career; it was also her brother who was the tyrannical father's scapegoat, who turned to drugs in his teens and was paternally immured in a mental hospital, where his poetic gifts were extinguished by repeated electroshock treatments. This marking story was recounted lyrically by Khoury-Ghata in 1998 in *Une maison au bord des larmes* (*A House on the Edge of Tears*)— one of only two of her seventeen novels which eschews fictional invention for autobiographical material. This novel shares the counterpoint present in all of Khoury-Ghata's poetry, between the immediate lyric or narrative and the backdrop of contemporary history—the history of war-torn Lebanon. In the construction of the poet's personal myth of origins, it was the silencing of the gifted, vulnerable brother that gave his sister access to the written word. (In the same year as Khoury-Ghata published *Une maison au bord des larmes*, her sister, the journalist May Ménassa, who stayed in Lebanon and writes in Arabic, published a novel on the same subject. Neither sister knew of the other's project before the books appeared.)

Khoury-Ghata's work bridges the anti-lyrical surrealist tradition which has informed modern French poetry since Baudelaire and the parabolic and communal narrative with its (we might say Homeric) repetitions of metaphors and semi-mythic tropes of poetry in Arabic. There are many French and Francophone poets of Arab—some of Lebanese—origin: Georges Shéhadé, Salah Stétié, Mohammed Dib, Habib Tengour, Tahar Bekri, Abdelwahhab Meddeb; women poets such as Andrée Chedid, Nadia Tueni, Nohad Salameh, Rachida Madani and Amina Saïd. But Khoury-Ghata's work is unique in its synthesis of the quotidian and the fantastic, its conciliation of the narrative and the lyric. She is the author of thirteen books of poems, most of which have for implicit backdrop the language and landscape of the poet's mother country. Though she was raised bilingual, her mother tongue was Arabic, and her earliest writings were in that language. She maintains the link as a gifted translator of contemporary Arabic poetry into French, and as a valued commentator on and promoter of modern writing in Arabic. She has written: "Nourished by the two languages, I write in Arabic through the French language—when my poems are translated into Arabic, they seem to be returning to their original language. For years, my first drafts were written in both languages, the Arabic going from right to left on the page and the French from left to right: they crossed each other's paths in the middle. Twenty-eight years in Paris haven't cured me of my mother tongue: when there's a problem, I take refuge in it, and am surprised when the people with whom I'm speaking don't understand!"

As she oscillates between French and Arabic, Khoury-Ghata moves with equal fluidity between poetry and fiction, and, in her poems especially, between life and death. Death becomes another mode of life, an ironic one carried on six feet below our surfaces, where the dead, according to the poet's own mythology, and, not unlike Homeric shades, "nourish themselves on the smell of our bread, drink the steam rising from our water, live on our noises." According to Khoury-Ghata, even the word "death" is a cornerstone of her work, making its way into several titles. This began for her "in 1975 with the unbearable images of Lebanon drowned in its own blood. Cadavers were laid out on wooden planks to be shoved into ditches for common burial with the same movement as a baker putting bread into the oven." Death: daily bread for the Lebanese. "I felt guilty about transforming the dead into words, lining them up like lead soldiers on my pages, but I was incapable of turning to another subject. Five years later, this collective death gave way to an individual death, that of my husband, the father of my daughter. Death which I'd picked up and examined barehanded blew up in my face." Death has a double register in her poems. It is experienced on a personal level, the deaths of husband, mother, brother, but with the collective specter of 200,000 people dead in Lebanon during the war that marked the poet's youth serving as a chorus to the intimate tragedy, a tragedy which had its reprise in the 2006 Israeli invasion that claimed more than a thousand mostly civilian victims

Just as Khoury-Ghata's verbal imagination of the word, sentence, poetic line, and balance of sound and sense function fluidly between two languages, so does her writerly perception travel fluidly between genres: poetry and fiction, with a constant intercourse between the two. Khoury-Ghata is an inveterate storyteller. Even in conversation, the account of a trip to the flea-market at the Porte de Clignancourt with her daughter or of a trip to Sénégal with an international writers' delegation becomes a multileveled tale with detailed descriptions of character and landscape, merciless satire of every kind of officiousness, unexpected asides that recoup the story, and, indeed, connect the flea market to the writers' congress. When her anecdotes deal with the past, the listener never knows if the story's denouement will be someone's personal victory over obstacles—ill-starred love, childlessness, poverty, illness, war—or an act of violence, an unanticipated death. Her novels range from the historical picaresque (the varied fates of five Frenchwomen shipwrecked on the Algerian coast in 1802) to the familial (her brother's descent from emerging poet to addict silenced by electroshock and lobotomy in war-wracked Beirut) to the fantastic (a Mediterranean island where the dead cohabit with the living). They almost always deal, in some fashion, with a passage between Europe and the Middle East, and with the passage, equally two-way, between life and death. Her poems, composed for the most part in sequences, often have the quality of exploded narratives, re-assembled in a mosaic in which the reader has at least the illusion of being able to find a more linear connecting thread. But in the end, it is the design of the mosaic itself that is most memorable. The same themes which animate the fiction are predominant in the poems: the tension between movement/change and tradition/sources, with all that is positive and negative in both; the unceasing commerce between human beings and the rest of the natural world, and between the dead and the living; the independent, puissant, and transcultural life of words.

The reference to a Thou who may be at once a God and a human beloved (an avatar of love) which one finds in Rumi, in Hafiz, in Ghalib, is absent from Khoury-Ghata's poetry, marked though it is by Arabic and even Persian poetic traditions. The *mythologos* here is of humanity, a meta-humanity at once more circumscribed and larger than life. In the village of Khoury-Ghata's poems, angels may converse with sign-painters and a pomegranate tree hang about a housewife's back door like a recalcitrant child. But just as Muslims, Christians, and Jews unhierarchically cohabit the village of "The Seven Honeysuckle Sprigs of Wisdom," neither the angelic nor the vegetable orders seem more powerful or prescient than the modest mother in "Early Childhood" who puts the stars, clouds, and seasons in their places. There is no apparent God: the dead have no more of an insider's view of the universe's workings than the living. Indeed, in "The Seven Honeysuckle Sprigs of Wisdom," the dead coexist and cohabit with the living. The village cemetery is more or less the wrong side of town, a *barrio* of the ultimately disenfranchised, who triple up in their graves in hard times, and can disparage no one:

> Youssouf the cemetery caretaker accuses the dead of being
> sloppy
> they eat the saltpeter off the walls and don't sweep up the
> crumbs
> Behind that fence says the selfsame Youssouf, no one is at
> his best
> you'd need someone more dead than you are to have
> something to boast about

Much of Khoury-Ghata's poetry, as well as *Une maison au bord des larmes,* could be described by Audre Lorde's term "biomythography," which Lorde coined for her own narrative *Zami.* Lorde's book resembles the classical memoir/bildungsroman more closely than does anything in Khoury-Ghata's work. What they have in common is at once their ex-centricity: the West Indian child in the Bronx, the Lebanese writer in Paris, and the enracination of their texts in an historical macrocosm which is rarely specified and everywhere implied: in Khoury-Ghata's case, the war in Lebanon, the state of siege in her mother country that is everywhere reflected in her work, presaged in the texts going back to a time preceding it, which was the time of her childhood and adolescence. An American reader wonders—is there as much rage collecting behind the seeming bemused and ironic resignation in Khoury-Ghata's enigmatic fables as there is in Lorde's parables? Given her country's recent history, how can there not be? Yet it is nowhere made evident in the poems: rather, it aliments them with a condensed energy which is "furious" in the sense of the word's etymology: it illumines them from within with a contained, volcanic fire.

Lyric poetry in English since the Romantics at least also often depends upon a "fiction of the self" which is as much a narrative device promoting immediacy of identification as it is a response to any "confessional" impulse. Lorde's "biomythography" has an autobiographical focus (or the lyrical fiction thereof) shared by her poems. In Khoury-Ghata's poems the "I," any speaker or figure, first-person singular or otherwise, whom the reader can interpret as standing for the poet herself, is a "significant absence"(as Mallarmé called Rimbaud). The enigmatic "she" of the poem I took the liberty of entitling "Widow" (untitled in French, though the sequences keep their original titles) is as close as a reader comes. The trope of the lyric speaker is notably absent from much contemporary French (and even Francophone) poetry, as widespread as it is in fiction. Khoury-Ghata's exuberant use of narrative in poetry—sometimes a mythos of the self, but more often narrative in all its inventive bravura—has been an affirmative return to poetry's tale-telling sources, as strong in French as anywhere, while her surrealist, or magic realist, imagery honors the verbal shape-shifting familiar to readers of poetry in, or translated from, Arabic.

The point of view of the initially "familial" sequence, "Early

Childhood," is that of a "we," which at first seems to be the cohort of siblings, but which expands itself to include the children of an entire culture, or children in general, bemused and half-wild, bewildered and yet more in touch with the agonized universe in all its manifestations than their elders. (Several of the poems are dedicated to May Ménassa, the writer-journalist sister who shared Khoury-Ghata's real childhood.) But the numinous protagonist of "Early Childhood" is a mother who partakes at once of the terrestrial, angelic, and chthonic orders, who assumes herself on speaking terms with God and an assortment of angels.

> I write Mother
> and an old woman rises in the uncertainty of evening
> slips into a wedding dress
> stands on tiptoe on her windowsill
> calls out to the hostile city
> addresses the haughty tribe of streetlights
> bares her chest to the clocks
> shows them the precise site of her sorrow
> disrobes gently for fear of creasing her wrinkles
> and unsettling the air
>
> My mother had her own way of undressing
> as one would strip the medals from a disgraced general

She ventures no further in her waking life than the cast shadow of a dining room's lampshade, but wanders to the ends of the universe in her sleep. She has daily commerce with the dead, and if she has a lover, it is a poet she mistrusts deeply who has been defunct for a hundred years: is the child she fears he will engender her poet daughter, or her daughter's poems? How unexpectedly and deftly, though, the sequence's focus changes as it nears its end, alternating the first-person plural of the children for a "they" who have colonized the country, made pornographic usage of its trees, imposed a multicolored but alien language.

"The Seven Honeysuckle Sprigs of Wisdom," in contrast, although not devoid of ominous shadows, seems an almost Arcadian *Cahier d'un retour au pays natal*, to a village which may or may not ever have existed. Religion is gently mocked from the opening (the priest has gone off in pursuit of a crow who cawed in biblical Aramaic), but the coexistence of Christians, Muslims, and Jews is taken for granted

> The priest the rabbi and the imam invited to the poor man's table,
> brought him three tufts of their beards which he planted in his garden
> The three upside-down trees which grew nine months later
> cast their shade on the devil's house

—and the clergy bring no good to anyone.

Authority is mocked as well, though we cannot but admire the conscientious schoolmaster who tries out the letters of the Arabic alphabet for practical use before imposing them on the children. The trees speak Arabic too, and may not answer to their names in French. Khoury-Ghata describes this sequence as being her fantasia on a venerable rural Arab tradition of public storytelling about the neighbors, inventing and embroidering more and more outrageous and poetic lies. (The composition in *patois* of slightly scandalous rhymed oral poems about the butcher's doings with the baker's wife and the priest's pheasant-poaching was also a savory feature of village life in France up through the first half of the twentieth century.) Khoury-Ghata has used this probably universal proto-fictional pastime to create a poet's vision of sources—not individual this time, but collective, with diverse names, ages, religions, and genders, a source as multi-faceted and bilingual as the poet herself. "The Cherry-Tree's Journey" evolves like a single folk-tale with a pungent humor, ludic, but shadowed with tragedy (and the prescience of emigration and exile).

The sequence called "Words" elaborates an often-playful mythology of words themselves, or of "the word": neither the Logos nor only the words of French or Arabic, but of all languages. It is a myth of alphabets, of speech and writing, created simultaneously by human beings and by the natural world of which they are a part. Once attempted, this seems a natural, almost a requisite subject for a Lebanese poet: the first written alphabet is said to have originated with the Phoenicians, ancestors of the Lebanese. However, in Khoury-Ghata's's dawn of origins, the first words are not the tools of Phoenician sailors and merchants: they issue from and belong to birds, to stones, to children, to wolves, to the night sky:

> I'll tell you everything   there were five pebbles
> one for each continent
> large enough   to contain a child of a different color
> pebbles which:
> broke up into alphabets
> ate a different earth   on each continent

Her fable of origins continues with in personifications of letters of the Arabic and Roman alphabets, contrasted with those unknown antediluvian alphabets

> which didn't survive the rising of the waters
>   letters buried in their silicate vestments   become silenced
>   sounds in the
> silenced
>   silt

(The alphabet of the Phoenicians survived, at least sufficiently for its tablets to be objects of our study and imagination in museums.)

> . . . projectiles against the cemetery wall
> they broke up into alphabets
> ate a different earth   on each continent
> "Aleph" breathes from right to left
> to erase dunes and camel-drivers
> who count the stars with their heads in the sand
> twelve times in a row
> It's in "Ba"'s basin that the moon's menstrual blood is washed
> in the eternal copper
> when women on nocturnal terraces make rash vows
> "Tah" paces up and down land poor in grass and compassion
> all that counts is the gesticulations of the shadow which
> erases   writes
> erases   writes steps and passers-by

There are country alphabets and town alphabets
Tell me what words you use I'll tell you   the number of
    your cattle

"The Darkened Ones" was written during the 2006 war. Are
its plural speakers generations of the dead once more, or are
they displaced refugees fleeing their calcinated villages, their no
longer habitable city blocks? Are they Lebanese of past generations, "welcoming" newcomers to an overdetermined and perennial warscape? The poet has not written a text to be deciphered:
it establishes its own dramatic parameters, with a chorus of
women wringing out laundry providing commentary while their
equestrian daughters escape to live another way.

> their daughters who ride the mountain bareback smell the
> heavy stones and storms rolling on the slope
> books, they say, are the children of sorrow
> the peelings of peelings of the forest
> it's better to decipher the sweat on the loins' stretched
>   drum-skin
> and let a red mare's galloping resonate between your thighs

Vénus Khoury-Ghata's multiple poetic persona is at once the
young woman riding away, the perennial washerwoman's chorus commenting and aggrandizing the quotidian, the equally
perennial mourner, and, above all, like the writer herself, the
woman re-creating the world in her book.

Provoking Engagement
June Jordan's Naming Our Destiny

June Jordan's new book is an anthology of causes won, lost, moot, private and public, forgotten and remembered. Anyone who doubts the relevance and timeliness of poetry ought to read Jordan, who has been among the front-line correspondents for almost thirty years and is still a young and vital writer. So should anyone who wants his or her curiosity and indignation aroused, or wants to read a voice that makes itself heard on the page.

There are as many kinds of poetry as there are novels and plays. But some critics, who would not fault a novel of social protest for failing to be a novel of manners or a *nouveau roman,* seem to want all poetry to fit one mold. June Jordan epitomizes a particular kind and strength of American poetry: that of the politically engaged poet whose commitment is as seamlessly joined to her work as it is to her life.

What makes politically engaged poetry unique, and primarily poetry before it is politics? Jordan's political poetry is, at its best, the opposite of polemic. It is not written with a preconceived, predigested agenda of ideas and images. Rather, the process of composition is, or reproduces, the process of discovering how events are connected, how oppressions are analogous, how lives interpenetrate. Jordan's poems are strongest when they deal with interior issues, when she begins with a politics of the personal, with the articulate and colloquial voice of, if you will, "a woman speaking to women" (and to men) and ranges outward to illustrate how issues, lives, and themes are inextricably interconnected. One of the most powerful examples is "Poem About My Rights," first published in 1980, which begins as an interior monologue of a woman angry because, as a woman, the threat of rape and violence keeps her from going where she pleases when she pleases:

> . . . without changing my clothes my shoes
> my body posture my gender identity my age
> my status as a woman alone in the evening/
> alone on the streets/ alone not being the point
> the point being that I can't do what I want
> to do with my own body because I am the wrong
> sex the wrong age the wrong skin

But she moves from the individual instances to the laws defining rape, and from rape to other questions of violation:

> which is exactly like South Africa
> penetrating into Namibia penetrating into
> Angola and does that mean I mean how do you know if
> Pretoria ejaculates

then deftly to Nkrumah and Lumumba, also in the wrong place at the wrong time, and to her own father, who was at once "wrong" himself as a working-class black male in his daughter's Ivy League college cafeteria and an oppressor who defined his child by her deficiencies. When Jordan concludes this poem with a defiant challenge to anyone seeking to physically or ideologically circumscribe her, we believe her and have made leaps—possibly new ones—of consciousness.

She uses a similar technique of accumulating incident/fact/detail in "Gettin Down to Get Over," a poem for her mother which swells to a litany of praise for black women and the African American family. "Free Flight," another late-night stream of consciousness, though it stays closer to the "personal," builds momentum and depth with Whitmanesque inclusiveness to consider the humorously identical possibilities of consolation by a female or a male lover before settling on self-respect as the best way to get through the night.

Where Jordan is unlike Whitman is in her creation of a quirky, fallible persona (apart from her creation of personae that are clearly different from that of the poet), an alter ego by which readers accustomed to identifying the poet with the speaker of a poem may sometimes be taken aback, if not shocked.

Jordan plays skillfully with this post-Whitman, post-Williams but also post-Romantic expectation in "Poem From Taped Testimony in the Tradition of Bernhard Goetz," an ironically issue-oriented dramatic monologue which transcends its headline-bound issue. Jordan's speaker breathlessly appropriates to a black perspective the reasoning Goetz used to justify arming himself and firing on black youths in the New York City subway. Is a black woman who has suffered every kind of violence from ridicule and exclusion to invisibility, battery, and rape at the hands of whites also justified in assuming the worst and acting accordingly? Justified if she carries a gun and fires not on a racist cop or armed rapist but on the white woman beside her at an artists' colony dinner table whose loose-cannon talk was the last straw? The poem is at once horrifying and funny, as a tall tale is meant to be, and hard to dismiss (even if, "logically" a reader who rejected Goetz's reasoning would reject that of Jordan's speaker as well).

The inevitability and passion of this poem, as well as its wit, will keep it valid and readable after the "issue" of Goetz is forgotten. The connection between being spat at on the way to third grade, seeing a neighborhood friend beaten by the police, being ignored in a New England drugstore, and being raped in a college town may not necessarily be apparent to all white (or even black male) readers. It's to Jordan's credit that she concretizes the link by juxtaposition, with the accelerating energy of deceptively ordinary speech. From her opening she establishes not only her speedy and frenetic "I" but the "they" that is, more than any "I" the opposite of "thou": the "they" that, be its antecedent "blacks," "whites," "Jews," "Muslims," "women," or "men," is the essential evil agent in any prejudiced discourse. Describing an incident that was perhaps only an eye contact made or avoided, the speaker here is confused—paranoid, the reader might think—or is she?

> . . . I mean you didn't
> necessarily see some kind of a smile
> or hear them laughing but I could
>   feel
> it like I could feel I could always
> feel this shiver thing this fear take
> me over when I would have to come
>   into a room
> full of them and I would be by myself
> and they would just look at you know
>   what
> I mean you can't know what I mean
> you're not Black.

Of course Jordan's proposition is farcically surreal, exaggerated to show the fallaciousness of its white equivalent, absurd (as the murder of twenty-two black children in Atlanta, the murder of fourteen women students in Montreal, the murder of one homeless man in New York's 103 Street subway station, are absurd; they all died for being "they" to someone). Nonetheless, a reader somewhere will categorize Jordan as a rabble-rousing reverse racist, missing the point of her "Modest Proposal": the quantum leap from grievance to slaughter and the culturally triggered impulse to jump it.

How can a white critic say that a black poet has a spectacular sense of rhythm? Modestly, or courageously. Jordan writes (mostly) free verse. Many writers of free verse produce a kind of syntactically disjointed prose, expecting line breaks to provide a concentration and a syncopation not achieved by means of language. In Jordan's best poems there is a strong, audible, rhythmic counterpoint to the line breaks, a rhythm as apparent to the reader as it is to the auditor who hears the poet deliver them. This is true of her poems that have been set to music by Bernice Reagon of the a cappella group Sweet Honey in the Rock ("Alla Tha's All Right, but" and "A Song of Sojourner Truth"), but it's equally true of dramatic monologues like "The Talking Back of Miss Valentine Jones" and "Unemployment Monologue," and of the interior monologues evolving into public declaration, like "Poem About My Rights."

The fluid speech-become-aria quality of Jordan's free verse

poems also makes them difficult to quote, though never difficult to remember. They are not made of lapidary lines and epigrammatic stanzas. They gather momentum verbally, aurally. Most often, the effects of the voice and the statement are cumulative.

Why is this important? Because it fixes the poems in the reader's memory; because it makes these poems, even those on the most serious subjects, paradoxically fun to read. It is a reason for these texts to be written in verse, to be poetry. They are not fiction, journalism, essays or any other form of prose, even when they share qualities with these other genres. When Jordan's poems are unambiguous and straightforward, as well as when they are figurative, ironic, or complex, her words create a music, create voices, which readers must hear the way they were written: Her poems read themselves to us.

Like many contemporary poets, Jordan sometimes ventures back into fixed forms. There are five sonnets and a loose ghazal sequence among the forty-three new poems here. Unfortunately, in the new sonnets the poet too often uses grandiose statement and inflated diction as if they came with the form:

> From Africa singing of justice and grace
> Your early verse sweetens the fame of our Race.
> ("Something Like a Sonnet for Phillis Miracle Wheatley")

Or she seems tone-deaf to the meter, which may always be broken, but for a purpose:

> I admire the possibilities of flight and space
> without one move towards the ending of my pain.
> ("A Sonnet from the Stony Brook")

She can also come up with a gem of a line like "A top ten lyric fallen to eleven" to refer to a fading love affair. Still, it's a long way from her best work in fixed forms, such as "The Reception," which depicts vividly imagined characters and action in iambic pentameter quatrains:

> Doretha wore the short blue lace last night
> and William watched her drinking so she fight
> with him in flying collar slim-jim orange
> tie and alligator belt below the navel pants uptight.

" . . . I flirt. Damned right. You look at me."
But William watched her carefully
his mustache shaky she could see
him jealous "which is how he always be

at parties."

Some of Jordan's most successful poems are the farthest from polemic. They are vignettes, short dramatic monologues, observations of characters who may or may not be in some interaction with the narrator, like "Newport Jazz Festival," "Patricia's Poem," and "If You Saw a Negro Lady":

> sitting on a Tuesday
> near the whirl-sludge doors of
> Horn & Hardart on the main drag
> of downtown Brooklyn
>
> solitary and inconspicuous as plain
> and neat as walls impossible to
> fresco and you watched her self-
> conscious features shape about
> a Horn & Hardart teaspoon
> with a pucker from a cartoon
> she would not understand
>
> would you turn her treat
> into surprise
> observing
>
> happy birthday

"The Madison Experience" expands this quick-take technique into a fourteen-part sequence that is a tender and surprising love song to one swath of Middle Western America. Its clean primary colors and color-blind courtesy impress the poet (who nevertheless "went out / looking for traffic") as much as the juxtaposition of rain-washed fresh produce, a rally for Soweto and "fathers / for Equal Rights." As much as anything, Jordan appreciates an untroubled solitude:

> Above the backyard mulberry tree
> leaves a full moon

Not quite as high as the Himalaya
Mountains
not quite as high as the rents in
New York City
summons my mind into the meat and
mud
of things that sing

Jordan hints at but does not politicize an "incorrect" sexuality. There are love poems to men and love poems to women, to black and to white partners, poems in the aftermath of loving, poems on the erotic edge of friendship, love poems that (no surprise) broadcast mistrust, question the accepted definitions of relationships. There has been pressure in the past three decades on black writers and on feminist writers to put their personal lives on the line, or to make them toe one (revolutionary black heterosexual monogamy; radical feminist lesbian ditto). "The subject tonight for / public discussion is / our love," Jordan writes ironically in "Meta-Rhetoric." Her only manifesto on her private choices has been her refusal to let them be the subject of discussion, at once revealing and sufficiently circumspect to make either name-calling or roll-calling impossible.

Often the glancing, yearning glimpses through language are more suggestive, more erotic than a clear depiction would be. (The word "lesbian" occurs only once in Jordan's book: the poet "worried about unilateral words like Lesbian or Nationalist." The word "gay," usually but not always in reference to men, is positively stated and vindicated.)

Rape is a subject about which Jordan is unambiguous. It is not sexual in nature but violent, and it is, she illustrates, analogous to other forms of violence motivated by lust for power, by "thou" becoming "they." She is not speculating. She reveals that she has been raped twice: "the first occasion / being a whiteman and the most recent / situation being a blackman actually / head of the local NAACP" ("Case in Point"). Her poems reexamine these violations through description, through metaphor ("Rape Is Not a Poem") and through theory ("Poem About My Rights"). If there is a "silence peculiar / to the female" ("Case in Point"), it is that of the forcibly silenced. "Poem on the Road" reiterates, through other women's stories, that no racial combination explains or excuses sexual violence. I think the double betrayal of black-on-black assault makes her angriest.

Another depiction which is mercilessly specific is that of one particular black nuclear family: the poet's own, beleaguered from without, reproducing the conditions of oppression within. West Indian strivers (a postal worker and a nurse), her father tried to beat his "Black devil child" into submission while making sure she was educated for rebellion, while her mother personified both submission and endurance to her daughter. We meet these people on the first pages of *Naming Our Destiny* and are back in their kitchen in the last poem, written thirty years later. The effect is much that of reading a novel in which new points of view reveal different, complementary truths about a character or situation, culminating in "War and Memory," which delineates how the dynamics of what we now call a dysfunctional family woke a bright child to the power of words and the possibility of dissent.

A *Selected Poems* is a second chance for an author and for readers. Work gone out of print can be rediscovered, the development and evolution of themes and style underlined. Poems bound too closely to an outdated topicality, or ones which are simply not good enough, can be cut out, thus placing the best-realized work into sharper relief. There are deleted poems I miss in this book: from *Things That I Do in the Dark,* "Uncle Bullboy" and the second "Talking Back of Miss Valentine Jones"; from *Passion,* "For Lil' Bit" and especially the two "Inaugural Rose" poems; from *Living Room,* "To Sing a Song of Palestine" and "Notes Toward Home." There are also texts that upon rereading seem to be occasional pieces whose occasion has passed: "On Moral Leadership as a Political Dilemma," "Some People," "What Would I Do White?" (wear furs and clip coupons; this reader optimistically thinks a white June Jordan would still be more June Jordan than Ivana Trump) and "Memo." In the newer work, "Poem Instead of a Columbus Day Parade," "The Torn Sky," and "Take Them Out!" pose the same problem. The events are current, but the poems don't transcend the level of chants, captions or slogans:

> Swim beside the blown-up bridges
> Fish inside the bomb-sick harbors
> Farm across the contra ridges
> Dance with revolutionary ardor
> Swim/Fish/Farm/ Dance
> Nicaragua Nicaragua
> ("Dance: Nicaragua")

Likewise, printing the word "chlorofluorocarbons" nine times down a page, with an odd simile in the middle, is less informative about the destruction of the ozone layer than was last week's exchange of letters in *The New York Times,* and less productive of thought and action on the issue.

There are, in short, too many propaganda poems, where the activist's desire to touch every base, to stand up and be counted on every current issue, took precedence over the poet-critic's choice of what ought to be published, not in a newspaper or a flyer but in a book that will be kept, read, and reread. One need only compare Jordan's elegy for Martin Luther King Jr., which is entirely, though musically, public, with her poem for Fannie Lou Hamer—also a public figure, but this time a person Jordan knew well and worked beside. There's a life, a voice, no hagiography but a lively portrait in "1977: Poem for Mrs. Fannie Lou Hamer":

> Humble as a woman anywhere
> I remember finding you inside the laundromat
> in Ruleville
> lion spine relaxed/hell
> what's the point to courage
> when you washin clothes?
> one solid gospel
> (sanctified)
> one gospel
> (peace)
> one full Black lily
> luminescent
> in a homemade field
> of love.

This could have been a poem for an aunt/sister/mother (the feeling of blood tie is so strong) as well as a poem about any brave friend. The fact that its subject was also a public (now historical) figure gives it another dimension, and the poet a status she or he has rarely held in this country: someone who writes as an intimate of the makers of history, as an actor in significant events—and who also reminds us that the face of history can be changed to a familiar, to a family face.

One public issue with which Jordan has been closely associated in recent years and which has become a recurrent subject of her poetry is the conflict in the Middle East, including Lebanon, and the struggle of the Palestinian people for self-determination in the West Bank and elsewhere. It's an issue that has at times polarized some readers' responses to her work. I too have stopped myself to examine my own responses to texts like "Apologies to All the People in Lebanon," "Living Room," and "Intifada." What I find is that Jordan does in these poems what she satirizes and exposes in the Bernhard Goetz monologue: She creates an undifferentiated "they" with no stated antecedent, which embodies evil, or at least the evil done to the Palestinians. A reader familiar with the events will know that Jordan's "they" sometimes refers to the Lebanese Christian Phalangist militia, sometimes to the Israeli army, sometimes to the present Israeli government. Because these names do not appear, what the "they" represents becomes unspecified, a monolith. Once a name has been written it is more difficult to use it unilaterally: There is the Lebanese army and the Israeli army, and also the Israeli peace movement. There is a poem in Jordan's previous collection, *Living Room*, that expresses confusion and dismay at the paradox of Lebanese-on-Lebanese violence. There is also one envisioning peace and cooperation, dedicated to an Israeli peace activist. These weren't included in the present collection. A poet, a worker with words, should use those words to clarify, not to obfuscate.

The best American writing I've read about Vietnam has been by black and white veterans who were there (Yusef Komunyakaa's *Dien Cai Dau* is a moving recent example), not by anti-war activists who weren't. I think the best poetry of the intifada will be written by Palestinians (and perhaps by dissident Israelis)—and that a writer who is neither, who hasn't been there except by analogy, runs the risk of letting exhortation and indignation replace observation and introspection. Adrienne Rich's recent poems about the Middle East are essentially the meditations of an American Jew who finds herself implicated in the conflict whether she chooses to be or not. Therein lie the tension and interest of the poems. The source of Jordan's involvement may be equally specific, but we don't know what it is. She gives us catalogues of the atrocities "they" performed; she seems to have no questions and to know all the answers. I think it is necessary to add that I write this as a Jew who is sickened by the Likud-led government's historically overdetermined version of apartheid, who is also opposed to, and frightened by, the conflation of that government with "Jews" too easily made by some right- and left-wing lobbyists and politicians.

Jordan's Palestinians and Nicaraguans are too often one-dimensional hero/victims. Jordan's African Americans, small-town Middle Western whites, and long-distance Brooklyn lovers of any race or sex are complex, even when glimpsed quickly in a hardware store or from a cab crossing a bridge at midnight. In spite of rage and outrage, even a rapist is not "they" but "thou":

> . . . considering the history
> that leads us to this dismal place
> where (your arm
> raised
> and my eyes
> lowered)
> there is nothing left but the drippings
> of power and
> a consummate wreck of tenderness/I
> want to know
> Is this what you call
> Only Natural?
> ("Rape Is Not a Poem")

The desire to reread and to pass a book on to others are two strong strands of a writer-reader connection. I don't know how many times I've read Jordan's work to myself and out loud to friends and students. At a writers' conference in Grenoble last

November I read "Poem About My Rights" to illustrate that North American feminist poetry could not be segregated from a tradition of politically engaged writing, and also to show how a poet could create a voice that would be heard as intended, no matter who was reading the poem. What is it about June Jordan's work that I like as much as I do? Its capacity to unsettle and disturb me, for one thing, to make me want to pursue the discussion, write something in response. In "War and Memory" she recounts that, as a child, she related the suffering of Jewish concentration camp prisoners—described factually by her father and symbolically, to epitomize women's specific pain, by her mother—to the war and internal bleeding in her home. The two-way trajectory between reporting and metaphor, between personal and global politics, is floodlit in Jordan's writing. Engaged as she is with the issues of the day and the irreducible issues of human life, her work provokes engagement with the reader, something too few readers now expect of poetry, something June Jordan gives back to poetry generously.

Unauthorized Voices

U. A. Fanthorpe and Elma Mitchell

It's more than a bit daft that the small (everyone admits and deplores the smallness) community of readers of poetry in English should have such difficulty finding each other, and finding the books that are the members' common interest and sustenance. Scottish salmon and Canadian cheddar cross borders more readily than books of verse. British ale is better traveled internationally than the work of most living British poets. American writers have perhaps fared better, but only marginally. Certain critics, with entrée into journals that do travel, promote the work of certain writers, certain chapels, certain publishers, all worth knowing about, but not representing, by any means, the range of what that already-small reading public abroad might come to know

As an American reader, my knowledge of contemporary British (to take that one example) poetry is haphazard, based on chance encounters between reader and book: books borrowed, books browsed in shops in England (where I lived for five years, and still visit), discoveries in periodicals and anthologies, the recommendations of friends: almost not at all, that is to say, on what I've found in American bookshops or through the American critical press. The poets I've discovered, putting myself in the way of happy accidents in Compendium or Silver Moon or the (London) Poetry Society Bookshop, are mostly not arcane, nor are they published by ephemeral presses. But Val Warner, Tony Harrison, Carol Ann Duffy, Tom Paulin (just to name a few) came to my notice only because of the good taste of the British booksellers who stocked them.

It was in 1984, not in a bookshop, but at a lecturer's desk at the University of East Anglia, that I happened, because I was waiting for someone, and they were on the desktop, to pick up *The Poor Man in the Flesh,* by Elma Mitchell, and *Side Effects,* by U. A. Fanthorpe, both unexceptional-looking slim volumes with covers uniform enough to let me know they were from the same publisher. I leafed first through *The Poor Man . . .* and found "Thoughts After Ruskin":

> Women reminded him of lilies and roses.
> Me they remind rather of blood and soap.
> Armed with a warm rag, assaulting noses,
> Ears, neck, mouth and all the secret places.
>
> Armed with a sharp knife, cutting up liver,
> Holding hearts to bleed under a running tap

Some pages later, there was the unflinching caritas of "Alice Uglier":

> Alice is uglier now by several years
>   Her eyes
> Are sunk and fortified against surprise,
>   Humiliations, tears.
> Sensible to the bone, her gait proclaims.
>   Her cut
> Of coat disdains the sympathiser, but
>   Her mouth is restless: tensions dug
>   These trenches in her throat.

Elma Mitchell, I learned to my surprise from the title page, was not a Hampstead companion of Fay Weldon's, but a sixty-five-year-old librarian living in Somerset, and this was her first book, published in 1976. Leafing through *Side Effects* (whose title is a wordplay on pathologies and points of view), I found a coherent setting seldom observed in poetry: that of a hospital seen from its underside: nurses, cleaners, and orderlies, in-and out-patients, the routine, the separations, the stasis, with the unifying voice that of an observer neither in danger nor in power, an underling: the Clerk's Tale:

Tomorrow these names will turn nasty,
Senile, pregnant, late,
Handicapped, handcuffed, unhandy,
Moribund, muddled, mute,

Be stained by living. But here,
Orderly, equal, right,
On the edge of tomorrow, they pause
Like giftbearers on a frieze

With the proper offering,
A time, a number, a name.
I am the artist, the typist;
I did my best for them.
                    ("The List")

Sometimes the individuals, patients or employees, speak.

She stands between us. Her dress
Is zipped up back to front.
She has been crying her eyes
Dark. Her legs are thinner than legs.

She is importunate

I'm not mental, am I?
Someone told me I was mental,
But I lost me memory
'Cos our dad died.
It doesn't make sense though, do it?
After I've been a nurse.
    ("Casehistory: Julie (encephalitis)")

Sometimes they achieve a collective voice:

The trolley's rattle dispatches
The last lover. Now we can relax
Into illness, and reliably abstracted
Nurses will straighten our sheets,

Reorganize our symptoms. Outside
Darkness descends like an eyelid.
It rains on our nearest and dearest
In car-parks, at bus-stops.
        ("After Visiting Hours")

U. A. Fanthorpe (I read) worked as a clerk in a Bristol hospital; she (Ursula) was only nine years Mitchell's junior, and this was a first book too. When my friend—an American poet-professor, exchange-teaching for a year—came to fetch me for my talk to her students, I was enthralled in reading. "I meant to show you those," she said. "They've both got more recent books out, too." It seemed that there was an undercurrent of feminist poetry in England, outside the women's movement literary circles (I would have heard of Fanthorpe and Mitchell, probably, had they been part of this new canon) and outside the circle of anthologized mid-career British poets (some of whom, like Harrison, Geoffrey Hill, Fleur Adcock, James Fenton, have excited my admiration and imagination) too.

I would call the poetry I read that day "feminist" because its largest concern appeared to be the re-vision of history through the perspective of the historically powerless and silenced: first, ordinary women, but also Mitchell's "Fisher Willie in Hospital":

> Not, as he seems, asleep,
> Eyeshut he lies and sees
> No fluorescent strip
> But restlessness of water
> Where the brown, bladdering weed
> Shaggies the reef.

(the limbo of hospital, or furnished room, where the individual is pared to essentials, is a frame returned to often by both these poets) and Fanthorpe's "Men on Allotments":

> As mute as monks, tidy as bachelors,
> They manicure their little plots of earth.
> Pop music from the council house estate
> Counterpoints with the Sunday morning bells,
> But neither siren voice has power for these
> Drab solitary men who spend their time
> Kneeling, or fetching water, soberly,
> Or walking softly down a row of beans.

—men who share, through chance or choice, temporarily or finally, the traditional powerlessness, or the traditional enracination in routine, assigned to women. Even on first, hurried reading, these were both poets who endeavored to speak from and to human conditions usually not given literary voice. There is seldom bravado or mere ventriloquism in their observations or adaptations of dramatis personae: they both observe carefully, and listen well, and respect what they report.

I intend the word "feminist" to describe, not to circumscribe, the work of these two writers. They are both poets who, I believe, envision a larger possible audience than that usually vouchsafed contemporary poetry: not an audience of women only, but not an audience predominantly made up of creative writing students (I would like to imagine that Elma Mitchell does not know what the initials MFA stand for), Old, New, or Post-Modern critics either: rather, an audience of novel readers, newspaper readers, ordinary readers. Fanthorpe twists her irony twice in the two stanzas of "Patience Strong," in which she first deplores the cynically versified inspirational pablum printed above that clearly bogus signature in British daily tabloids and Sunday magazines, and then depicts "a working-man, a fellow in his fifties" in "epileptic outpatients," who confides of such verse, "This is what keeps me going." Even if the middle-aged epileptic thwarted in his desire to join the ambulance brigade reminded this reader of the New York Sunday paper's Hundred Neediest Cases, Fanthorpe's subtextual assessment of the contemporary poet's possible, often neglected, aspiration, is there. The working man is reading "Patience Strong" at least in part because Hughes, Fuller, Heaney, and Tomlinson—and Fanthorpe herself—have not given him what he needed, even when he knew that what he needed was poetry; or because they have, in some other way, been made inaccessible to him.

There is no question in my mind that U. A. Fanthorpe would like to be read by the sort of people she writes about: the patients, clerks, and nurses, the first-year students, the frowsy women dons, the balding gardener, the irascible heroic friend reading Cowper while he endures cancer treatment. Nor are Mitchell's suburban retirees, boardinghouse office workers, middle-aged widows, being scrutinized for a tweedier audience with ice clinking in a glass. The Leeds-born poet Tony Harrison, while writing brilliantly of his working-class origins, despairs that they are being "served up in sonnets for the bourgeoisie." U. A. Fanthorpe and Elma Mitchell—who are not working-class poets in the sense that Harrison is—by birth—do not share that despair, and are not, except exceptionally, addressing the bourgeoisie over their shoulders when they have chosen other subjects.

They have this in common with many American poets, whose work they may or may not have read, who seek, as well, interaction with an Other who is at once subject and reader. Black poets who make their art of the particularities of black life and language, the poets of the women's movement who examine the contradictions of the human/female quotidian, are (among others) writing, first of all, for those of whom they speak. And almost all love poetry conflates its subject/object with its ideal reader. But often, and not always to its detriment, such poetry has among its aims that of teaching, preaching, convincing: to show the black/female/gay/Asian, etc., reader both the values and the inequities that may be subsumed in habit; to let other readers know that such subjects are sentient Subjects, to be ignored at their own risk, and to make them part of the roused indignation; or, more directly, to persuade the beloved of the lover's desirability and sincerity. At its best, this is artistic engagement; at its worst, it is (even if you agree with the writer) polemic or propaganda.

Reading Fanthorpe or Mitchell, I do not get the sense that either one is trying to talk me into anything, or that if the Sunday gardener, the orderly, the boardinghouse cleaning woman, did read these poems, they would be moved to anything but the very ordinary and incomparable epiphany that their lives are worth looking at, living, and writing about, and that, written about, this is how they read:

> I come in with the Hoover
> And the eleven-o-clock in the morning light
> (Which he never sees)
> Blanching his unmade bed
> And all the things he has left me in his wilfulness—
>
> Fragile constructions of ash,
> A glass that contained something totally odourless,
> An uninteresting wastepaper basket
> And a fortune in tea-leaves.
> (Elma Mitchell, "Service Provided," *Furnished Rooms*)

Since Mitchell and Fanthorpe write so often about ordinary "undistinguished" people, in a style too readable to be called experimental, and since neither they nor their subjects claim the interests of a specific class, race, ethnicity, or political stance as parti pris, an American critic might be tempted to call them, like the people of whom they write, "modest" or "middle-range." This would be doing them a disservice, because, in the critical vocabulary applied to poetry, these words imply mediocrity, stylistic limitations, and sentimental excess, rather than reticence and fine observation. They are modest in the manner of Pym or Powys, a self-imposed modesty we Americans more often associate with novelists, who are entitled to pick a locale, a particular subgroup of the human species for their observations, inventions, and obsessions. These two poets are modest in the manner of Philip Larkin, who did become familiar to American readers, and if neither of them exercises his technical bravura, they have, both, a largesse of spirit, manifested by intellectual curiosity and a compassion untinged with condescension that was largely foreign to him. The parts of the world and its inhabitants that they are regarding are very similar, but Fanthorpe and Mitchell are looking more outward than inward; and their self-reflection, when it is there, although it can be blunt, and looks into the abyss more than once, refuses despair.

> When we were turning out the mattresses,
> Fooling and laughing and heaving and calling across,
> I suddenly remembered: you aren't here.
> And stood, shaken to pieces by the loss;
> As we were turning out the mattresses,
> I had to go on. Irreparable distresses,
> Eloquent elegies, the waste of tears
> Aren't for women with supper to get and all.
> (Elma Mitchell, "Turning Out the Mattresses," *People Etcetera)*

Mitchell's poems give no more internal indication, in fact, that this bereavement is "the poet's" than the motherhood or celibacy, handicaps or occupations of which she also writes.

While Mitchell frequently alludes to the strength tapped from the life force of routine necessities and occupations, especially women's traditional occupations, cooking, cleaning, renewing, continuing, Fanthorpe's situations *in extremis* are relieved by the more Roman consolations of philosophy, literature, connection with a written tradition:

> . . . More symptoms, and his friends come, go, come, go,
> Swallowing hereafters,
>
> And he transacts the same
> Miniature feats of gallantry with which
> Cowper restrained the dark
>
> Once, as far as we know
> ("Tomorrow and," *Selected Poems*)

> . . . I catch you
> House-training the dragon, my absence, with small
> Jokes, diet of liver and onions, digging
> A vegetable patch, reading my old books.
>
> Why, I ask, why the Anglo-Saxons?
>
> Because, you said, they understand exile.
> ("Difficilior lectio," *A Watching Brief*)

Neither Mitchell's nor Fanthorpe's poems are literary exemplars of Good Works, to be read for their salutary effect on our spiritual health. If they are capable of discerning tragedy in ordinary lives and events, they also find there humor, beauty, epiphany. This is the conclusion of Fanthorpe's "Men on Allotments":

> . . . . Cabbages
> Unfurl their veined and rounded fans in joy
> And buds of sprouts rejoice along their stalks.
> The ferny tops of carrots, stout red stems
> Of beetroot, zany sunflowers with blond hair
>
> And bloodshot faces, shine like seraphim
> Under the long flat fingers of the beans

They can be wryly or wickedly funny, they can each make a rich and precise poetic diction seem as transparent as a shopping list, or a short note from a frank and literate friend. The reader is grateful for such franchise, while never questioning that what is on the page is not improvised, but the result of craft and attention.

Gardening, reading Cowper, or turning out the mattresses, they are both "very English," which means that certain locutions, rituals, place-names and social cues may be unfamiliar to some American readers—those who have never crossed the threshold of the kind of British fiction that makes remarkable the lives of unremarkable people in unremarkable places: Jane Austen, Mary Webb, Thomas Hardy. In any case, Americans don't balk at Mississippi "regionalism' because we live in Iowa, or reject the specificities of Harlem because we know only those of the Mission District.

Fanthorpe is less wary of the (discreetly) autobiographical element in her poetry than is Mitchell. Like the even more reticent Marguerite Yourcenar, whose "memoirs" range backwards through the histories of her paternal and maternal grandparents, stopping short on the day after her own birth, Fanthorpe creates a "self," a persona, that is, of the poet/speaker, not so much by depicting that adult self in situation and action, or even by re-creating that self as adolescent or child, as by realizing the personages and influences molding that self: father, mother, brother, school:

> My extrovert dog of a father
> With his ragtime blazer and his swimming togs
> Tucked like a swiss roll under his arm
> Strides in his youth towards us down some esplanade,
>
> Happy as Larry. You, on his other arm,
> Are anxious about the weather forecast,
> His overdraft, or early closing day.
> ("Fanfare," *Selected Poems*)
>
> . . . Overhead the patter of tiny
> Paws or dense whirring of wings.
> There were more humans around, too
>
> Than you quite expected, living furtive
> Separate lives in damp rooms. Meals, haphazard
> And elaborate, happened when, abandoning hope,
>
> You had surrendered to bread
> And butter. . . .
> ("My Brother's House," *Selected Poems*)

Always autumn, in my memory.
Butter ringing in the drilled teashop crumpets;
Handmade chocolates, rich enough to choke you,
Brought in special smooth paper from Town.

(Back at school, the square tall piles
Of bread, featureless jam in basins,
Grace, a shuffle of chairs, the separate table
For the visiting lacrosse team.)

Long afternoons in hotel lounges,
Islanded in swollen armchairs, eyeing
Aristocratic horses in irrelevant magazines.
Should I be talking to Them?
                    ("Half-Term," *Selected Poems*)

A lover/life companion is most movingly limned in and by
her absence, or by her reaction to the speaker's absence: not
abandonment or betrayal, simple quotidian absences caused by
work or family responsibilities ("Chaplaincy Fell Walk," "Diffi-
cilior Lectio"). In "At Aversham" (*A Watching Brief*), the lover
re-creates the beloved and their connection through the evocation of their fathers, small boys who lived four miles apart,
but never met:

Here my four-year-old father opened a gate
And cows meandered through into the wrong field.

I forget who told me this. Not, I think,
My sometimes reticent father . . .

Your father, pampered only brother
Of many elder sisters, four miles away

Grew up to scull on this river. My father,
Transplanted, grew up near poets and palaces . . .

So here I stand, where ignorance begins,
In the abandoned churchyard by the river,

And think of my father, his mother, her father,
Your father, and you. Two fathers who never met,

Two daughters who did . . .

It is only specified, thus understatedly, in Fanthorpe's most recent book, *A Watching Brief,* that these two faithful companions are both women: a pronoun, a noun: a revelation that perhaps took more courage on the poet's part because it was not being made as a stance, or a political statement. Although it is one nonetheless.

(Fanthorpe was born in the same year as Adrienne Rich; Mitchell, as May Swenson.)

Elma Mitchell, on the contrary, continues to eschew, or elude, self-revelation. Her 1983 book, *Furnished Rooms,* is a tour de force of thirty-six poems in the personae of boarding-house occupants in some unspecified English city. They are middling—displaced souls who find themselves, or who have chosen to be, living each within four anonymous walls in an accidental noncommunity: widower, widow, restive youth, girl trying on faces, a divorced mother, a runaway husband, a lesbian couple, a nightclub hostess, an old mother and her aging daughter, a half-cracked artist oblivious of anything beyond her handiwork:

> I came a widower
> To this dull room.
> The castle had collapsed
> Without a housekeeper,
> She sat beside my bed
> In her wedding dress
> Smiling and smiling
> Apprehensively
> Through glass.
> ("Bluebeard's Castle")

It's mother, you see.

I cannot fold her up like a pram or a bicycle.
It's every day crawling around the agencies.
I cannot leave her alone in a furnished room.
She has to come with me, arm in arm, umbrella'd
Or trailing a little.
("It's Mother, You See")

It is late in the day
(It is always late in the day)
To quarrel with footsteps chattering down the stairs
Not stopping at my door
It is now in the day
(Saturday now in the day)
To lie in an unmade bed, by a splattered pane
And watch the waterdrops
Collect
  Collide
    Connect
    ("In Youth Is Pleasure")

What harm can I do with clay?
Dirty stuff, they say,
Well, messy, anyway.
But I've taken down the curtains,
Rolled back the carpet, stripped the bed and hidden
The pictures somewhere—

I squat on the floor
And men come out of my fingers
And beasts, and things
I wouldn't give a name to.
    ("Sculptress")

Less than any other does the voice, again, of bereavement require, among these fleshed vignettes, any other costume but its
intensity:

You left this world and I said Shortly
It'll be winter how time flies
These days or crawls
Like flies

You left this world I say you left
My tongue tied
My left side
Cold.
  ("Left")

In her most recent published work, Mitchell undertakes Biblical personae: Adam, Eve, the accuser of the woman taken in adul-

tery, Jesus informing anachronistic reporters that "The Crucifixion Will Not Take Place." For me, the most successful of these is
"The Death of Adam," another poem about bereavement. Eve,
watching her spouse grow old and feeble, reminds the reader
that every person becoming conscious of, observing, the decline
of a loved one, is a "first person" seeing it for the first time:

> Teeth fall out, and then the face falls in.
> Skin
> Withers and wrinkles and shrivels like an apple
> (Yes, like an apple)
> And the top of the skull
> (Where the hair and the brains keep complicated house
> together)
> Becomes
> Plain, smooth, simple,
> Unoccupied by anything.
>
> And he couldn't walk at all, nor talk at all
> (We had to stop arguing about whose fault it was)
> And the sun made his eyes hurt
> . . . .
> . . . must I look forward
> To a separate, feminine, suitable
> Method of disapearance?
> Middle-aged, but still naked
> To man-stare and God-stare,
> Covering myself up with my hands and my long grey hair,
> Breasts falling like apples
> And the small pool of darkness
> Inside me
> Gone dry?

Fanthorpe has also created "unauthorized versions" of Biblical, historical, and literary subjects. Her New Testament piece
(dedicated to Mitchell) is spoken by Mary, the sister of Lazarus
and Martha, defending the latter against historical calumny certain to come in the wake of her "monumental dressing-down" by
"Josh." "What poor old Mart could have done with / Was a mirac-
ulous draught of coffee and sandwiches / Instead of a ticking-
off." For both of these poets, Judeo-Christian tradition is a

source of folk-tale material, to be used anecdotally, dressed in contemporary clothes and diction, for the purpose, almost inevitably, of debunking some hierarchy. The poems that do approach the spiritual, the metaphysical, the Umwelt, dealing with death, the individual's relation with a larger humanity, with the past, with the possibility of continuity or extinction, draw their figurative language from nature and from human construction, from recorded human history and literature, and, especially for Fanthorpe, from Greek, Roman, and Egyptian tradition. In her second book, Fanthorpe attempted "revisions" of a group of Shakespearean female characters; she also lent a voice to the much-maligned Person (an acrostic-writing clergyman) from Porlock. Perhaps the most fully realized, certainly the most ambitious of her dramatis personae is the nameless World War I veteran of "The Constant Tin Soldier," who ends his life as a traveling salesman, dissatisfied with children, wife, adopted town, longing for "the formal beauty of rank" that was destroyed forever for him in one predawn disarrayed and bloody retreat in 1918.

A recent group of poems enlarges the dramatic monologue to synthesize perceptions of literary and historical figures with those of the poet/speaker. It is only fitting that a poet whose work resonates with voices of the common woman and man should revise the Wordsworth canon:

> Years later William knocked it together;
> Mary gave her two lines. But it was Dorothy
> Did the fieldwork, across the daffodilled years,
> On a threatening misty morning. April
> 1802. A boat is floating in the middle
> Of the bay. Cows cause a diversion.
> They see the yellow flower that Mrs. C.
> Calls pilewort; wood-sorrel; daffodils, naturally.
>
> Waves at different distances, and rain
> And a sour landlady (it is her way)
> And excellent ham and potatoes. Warm rum
> And water for two—seven shillings all told.
> We enjoyed ourselves, she says, and wished
> For Mary.
>
> ("Deer in Gowbarrow Park," *A Watching Brief*)

As of 1988, Elma Mitchell has published four books: *The Poor Man in the Flesh* (1976), *The Human Cage* (1979), *Furnished Rooms* (1983), and *People Etcetera: Poems New and Selected* (1987), all published by Peterloo Poets in Cornwall. U. A. Fanthorpe is the author of five: *Side Effects* (1978), *Standing To* (1982), *Voices Off* (1984), *Selected Poems* (1986), and *A Watching Brief* (1987). They were also all published by Peterloo, but the paperback of *Selected Poems* appeared as part of the King Penguin series, an important recognition and opportunity for an extended readership.

Peterloo Poets is a small press in Cornwall, run by Harry Chambers, that has been in existence for about fifteen years, during which Chambers has published over a hundred titles, eighty-two of which are still in print. He is now bringing out ten or twelve a year, all poetry, for the most part collections by individual writers; for the most part, poets who had not previously been published in book form elsewhere, though many, once published by Peterloo, have multiple titles there. There are more women than on any British poetry list I know, excepting those of the women's presses (which don't publish that much poetry). Chambers doesn't seem to adhere to any literary school or rule: he publishes the poets whose work appeals to him, however he finds them, or they find him. I know of hardly any other presses in England, Ireland, or the United States that publish only poetry, that publish so many titles, and that seem to try so hard to keep those titles in print and in circulation. Copper Canyon in Port Townsend, Washington, Alice James Press in Cambridge, Massachusetts, and Naomi Long Madgett's Lotus Press in Detroit, publishing African American poets for the past near-twenty years, are among the few in this country that come to mind.

I took the liberty of writing to Elma Mitchell (in Somerset) and Ursula Fanthorpe (in Gloucestershire), and in order to make them more present to American readers of this article, asked each how she would locate herself as a poet, as a woman writer, as a poet whose work only began to be widely published when she was in her forties/fifties, and how this came to happen. They both responded generously, like any wordsmiths, elaborating and eliding as they chose.

Elma Mitchell

I was born in 1919 in Airdrie, Lanarkshire, Scotland, in a predominantly industrial area, which remained my home until 1941, although I spent a good part of each year away from home, in residence at a girls' boarding school in Surrey, England, and then from 1938 to 1941 at Somerville College, Oxford.

In 1941, i.e. the early years of World War II, after graduation from Oxford, I came to London and started work for the British Broadcasting Company, and after the war I continued living and working in London, mainly in publishing. I trained and qualified as a librarian at University College, London, and have worked also in that capacity.

In 1961, I came to live permanently in the depths of rural Somerset, with friends with whom I had lived throughout the war and post-war years in London; I have worked here as poet, translator, free-lance critic and general dogsbody.

I have read and written poetry from early childhood, but published nothing (apart from fortunately extinct verses in school and college magazines) until the late 1960s, and then only stray pieces in magazines and anthologies. I had tried my hand at short-story writing (and had one broadcast), but I realized I had neither passion nor talent for narrative, and my perceptions of people came out more naturally in poems. In 1969, a collection of poems, *Seasons and Enquiries* (title from a notice above a railway ticket-office in London), won a competition for an unpublished collection. It remains unpublished, though some of the better poems have appeared in my later volumes. Thereafter, I came into contact with Harry Chambers of Peterloo Poets, always on the lookout for new poets, and he has been my publisher ever since.

Few of the poems are strictly autobiographical, but they are of course based on years of observation and recollection from the London years and after.

I am not sure that I am any kind of "ist," but yes, of course I write as a woman poet, with a woman's mind and perceptions and experience and reactions—and body! I loved and still love Scotland, but had to look elsewhere for the work I wanted; I thoroughly enjoyed student life and London life; to these I owe much in the way of interesting work and lasting friendships; and enduring images of people etc. But I am equally happy in the country, with quiet and peace, congenial company, and poems still coming on! (I was born in a house with a railway station and a town in front, and fields and hills at the back—perhaps that explains everything! or not).

"Thoughts After Ruskin" (published 1967) remains my most popular and most feminist poem.

U. A. Fanthorpe

Who I feel myself to be as a writer: Important that I began as a clerical assistant—a very low rank in the National Health Service—in a hospital where the top jobs were held by men. I thus began by feeling that I wrote for and about the voiceless: the patients, the cleaning women. I felt very strongly that I wanted to be subversive: saw myself as being against power-holders, with no weapons except words and laughter.

As a woman poet: This seems a pertinent question. I was conscious that being a woman was another way of being on the "wrong side"—but it was also an encouragement, because I felt quite often that, as men don't have such lowly jobs, I had exceptional chances in the things I saw, and that—with any luck—the voice and the feelings that I had would be understood by women. I saw myself not just as a woman writer, but as finding an audience of women, and saying things that women would understand. By this I don't however mean that I have a "programme" to follow—the poems come and exert their own authority. It's no good thinking "this is what I ought to write": what I'm really concerned with is getting it right, telling the truth, letting the poem say what it wants to say.

As a poet whose first books were published in my forties: Felt great joy! Much better than starting young. It was something I'd always wanted—and here it was happening when I no longer hoped for it. It was a rebirth of a most wonderful kind.

How did it come to happen: By giving up teaching (which had drained away my creative energies) and by having a really low status job.

These things left me free to think my own thoughts. Practically, it was enormously helpful to have a forty-minute lunch break (just long enough to begin writing) and to be allowed to have it in a disused caravan, where I was alone. It was, I suppose, very much a matter of time and space.

I hope that American readers—and editors—will have the time and space for these two eloquently accessible British poets.

Eloquent Ingloriousness
Tony Harrison's Selected Poems

The American publication of Tony Harrison's Selected Poems is cause for celebration. The copyright and trade conventions that have kept a poet as readable and accomplished as Harrison from American audiences until now are, on the contrary, to be deplored. What can provide a potentially popular novelist with a separate American (or British) contract often prevents the writer of a less "marketable" genre like poetry from being read across the ocean at all, unless the original publisher has a subsidiary in the other country.

So non-transatlantic British readers will have had no access to the work of, for example, May Swenson, Richard Howard, or Gwendolyn Brooks. And most American readers have not, until now, known of Tony Harrison.

Harrison is not a "new" poet, a particularly "young" poet (he is fifty), or a poet whose work requires the understanding of some abstruse aesthetic to be accessible. He brings to his poetry the experience and vocabularies of a specific life, place, class; that very specificity, rendered and orchestrated with consummate craft, is what opens his work to myriad possible readers. He creates, in his best poems, a reality as textured and well observed, as full of exterior events and interior change, as that of the most exuberantly nonminimalist fiction.

I once quipped that if the focus of lyric poetry is love, death, and the changing of the seasons, the novel's focus is love, death, and the changing of class. By that definition, Tony Harrison is a quintessential fiction-maker. What I return to most frequently in the work of this poet, so unlike myself, yet so similar in his assumption of difference, is the sonnet sequence "The School of

Eloquence," which occupies sixty-six pages of the present collection. It is an angry, funny, earthy, erudite poem, something between a bildungsroman and a novel of retrospection, recounted in sixteen-line Meredithian sonnets. A bright working-class boy from Leeds (father: bakery worker and former miner; mother: housewife) is educated to "rise beyond his class." His parents encourage him, even as his education, particularly the different spoken language it requires, separates him from them. As a young man, he becomes a writer; as a grown man, he realizes that the matter and substance of his art must be the very language above which he "rose," and its incorporation into literature: the occupation of literature by those it had excluded, silenced. But what he left has changed: His parents are old and are shocked by or indifferent to his outspoken work. His mother dies; his grieving father, uncomforted by an alien son, dies in his turn. Working-class northern row houses are occupied by immigrants with dark skins; unemployment, not the mines, blights young lives. Nothing is as it was and the living dialect recorded by the poet may, he realizes with irony, go the way of Cornish or Welsh: be a dead language or a literary preserve.

Harrison chooses the sonnet to tell this story for the same reason that many American poets have eschewed it: The fourteen-line (or Meredithian sixteen-line) verse paragraph or vignette, historically associated with courtly love, courtly flattery, and metaphysical speculation, and with a privileged and educated class, is not (they say) the vehicle for the poetry of those denied privilege, for the poetry of demotic utterance. But Harrison seizes the form precisely to embody his struggle with the language of "educated men." The sequence begins with a sonnet entitled "On Not Being Milton," which makes poetry from the challenge of the unspoken:

> the looms of owned language smashed apart!
> Three cheers for mute ingloriousness!
> Articulation is the tongue-tied's fighting.
> In the silence round all poetry we quote
> Tidd the Cato Street conspirator who wrote:
>
> Sir, I Ham a very Bad Hand at Righting

Closure is a problem for many sonnet writers. When all but one or two lines demanded by the form are there, a tying-up is required; even in Shakespeare, sometimes the result is abrupt and seems obligatory. Harrison's closures are usually powerful, pulling together disparate, even warring elements in the poems (the first two quatrains above are intentionally neither mute nor tongue-tied) or, as in "Timer," using a metaphor or simile to knit up a discursive whole.

The struggle between demotic and elevated language is as often the subject of a poem as the parallel struggles between classes or generations:

> 4 words only of mi 'art aches and . . . "Mine's broken,
> you barbarian, T.W.!" He was nicely spoken.
> "Can't have our glorious heritage done to death!"
> I played the Drunken Porter in Macbeth.
> ("Them & [uz]")

> And so the lad who gets the alphas works
> the hardest in his class at his translation
> and finds good Ciceronian for Burke's
> *a dreadful schism in the British nation.*
> ("Classics Society")

Often, in formal poetry, language becomes a collaborator in the creative process, with the necessity of finding a rhyme, an iamb, or an assonance prodding the poet to open linguistic files otherwise shut. In Harrison's sonnets, the transmutations and implications of language itself—English versus Latin, dialect versus "standard" English—are the impetus to poetry and provide several linguistic veins to be mined.

The love and death in "The School of Eloquence" are the poet's rediscovered love for, and the deaths of, his parents, viewed initially, once again, through the lens of language-as-difference. Their language was what the young poet had to forswear to become a poet, but it is what he must reclaim in order fully to realize his gift. Moving between two modes of diction, he discovers that this motion is his true subject. But in the poems about "mi mam" and "mi dad," neither theory nor sentimentality obscures the individuals portrayed, in relation to their son or to each other. The widowed father, in particular, is made real, though not reconciled, to his son through grief:

> You're like book ends, the pair of you, she'd say.
> Hog that grate, say nothing, sit, sleep, stare. . .
> The "scholar" me, you worn out on poor pay,
> only our silence made us seem a pair.
> Not as good for staring in, blue gas,
> too regular each bud, each yellow spike.
> A night you need my company to pass
> and she not here to tell us we're alike!
> Your life's all shattered into smithereens.
> Back in our silences and sullen looks,
> for all the Scotch we drink, what's still between's
> not the thirty or so years, but books, books, books.
> ("Book Ends 1")

These 200-plus pages give the scope and distance of Harrison's development. He was a brilliant crafter from the start (*The Loiners*, published in 1970). He had gone to school to Catullus, Kipling, Browning, Auden, MacNeice; perhaps Robert Lowell had made an impression. The younger Harrison's work could be charged with bombast and self-indulgence, but never with inattention to craft. Plenty of verbal fireworks are exploded in these poems, and fire and fireworks are frequent images, associated, often in the space of a poem, with sex, pain, death, drunkenness, and epiphany. "The Nuptial Torches," one of the most powerfully realized earlier poems, is a dramatic monologue spoken (in iambic pentameter couplets) by Isabella, the young French bride of Philip of Spain, witnessing an *auto-da-fé* occasioned by a Spanish naval defeat and her wedding. Sex and violent death by fire are equally strange to her, equally imposed upon her, and, through the experience, inextricably linked:

> Young Carlos de Sessa stripped was good
> For a girl to look at and he spat like wood
> Green from the orchards for the cooking pots.
> Flames raveled up his flesh into dry knots . . .

The killing fire leads her, willing or not, to her husband's heat:

> O let the King be gentle and not loom
> like Torquemada in the torture room,
> Those wiry Spanish hairs, these nuptial nights
> Crackling like lit tapers in his tights,
> His seed like water splurted off hot stone.

This is Harrison's one assumption of a female persona in the lyric work (he is also the author of a *Phaedra Brittanica* set in India, and has translated the *Oresteia* and *Medea*, which he subtitled "A Sex-War Opera").

Burning, stench, and death lead to sex in "The Nuptial Torches"; they are linked, in the opposite order, in "Allotments," whose speaker's voice prefigures that of "The School of Eloquence." Again in couplets, the poem begins with Leeds's teenage lovers electrically groping each other in overgrown victory gardens, graveyards, behind the slaughter house:

> Stroked nylon crackled over groin and bum . . .
> And young, we cuddled by the abbatoir
> Faffing with fastenings, never getting far.
> Through sooty shutters the odd glimpsed spark
> From hooves on concrete stalls scratched at the dark
> And glittered in green eyes. Cowclap smacked
> Onto the pavement where the beasts were packed
> And offal furnaces with clouds of stench
> Choked other couples off the lychgate bench.
> The Pole who caught us at it once had smelt
> Far worse at Auschwitz and at Buchenwald,
> he said, and, pointing to the chimneys, Meat!
> Zat is vere zey murder vat you eat.

The speaker recalls how, his assignation and his dinner spoiled, he "cried / for the family still pent up in my balls, / for my corned beef sandwich, and for genocide." The reader doesn't know what's become of the young woman—gone home, equally horrified? Left standing there by her Swain—even though one "you" addresses the retrospection to her.

A certain masculine myopia ("Allotments" is one of the least egregious examples) characterizes Harrison's earlier work, full as it is of various more or less well realized male characters. For all of them, half of humanity seems to consist only of a series of breasts, bellies, and buttocks, of various shades and in various states of undress, all depersonalized, from the unfortunate

> Everything in this rich dark
> craves my exclamation mark.
> Wife! Mouth! Breasts! Thigh!
> ("The Heart of Darkness")

to the Kiplingesque civil servant's "taste" for Nigerian women in "The Songs of the PWD Man," or the author/speaker's desire for diversion in the Kremlin with an Intourist guide ("The Curtain Catullus"). British wife, unknown Russian or African, they are equally faceless exotics with no separate existence evoked by the poems, equally objectified. The prevalence of this makes the male personae hard to tell apart.

Ten years later, when the poet's work returns to Leeds and origins, how very different is this evocation of a woman/child miner:

> Among stooped getters, grimy, knackerbare,
> head down thrusting a 3 cwt corf
> turned your crown bald, your golden hair
> chafed fluffy first and then scuffed off
> . . . .
> Patience Kershaw, bald hurryer, fourteen,
> this wordshift and inwit's a load of crap
> for dumping on a slagheap, I mean
> th 'art nobbut summat as wants raking up.
> ("Working")

Similarly, the sensitivity with which Harrison observes his aging father's reaction to his new brown and black neighbors is extended to the neighbors themselves. The issue of population change and its attendant potential race conflict in a working-class community is confronted by the older poet, who reduced Africans to ornaments and orifices, invisible as sentient subjects, a decade earlier.

Since Harrison's work has not been available to readers this side of the Atlantic, his example of subverting and expanding the possibilities of received form with nonstandard English, and the issue itself of the relation of such form to nonstandard-English speakers, cannot be said to have influenced American writers. But some American poets are exploring parallel courses. The Chicano poet Alberto Ríos and black poets Cheryl Clarke and Marilyn Nelson come to mind; Derek Walcott, West Indian, resident in America by choice, has made stunning formal poetry in Caribbean patois, alongside the major body of his work in standard English. Joan Larkin's crown of sonnets about a working-class teen-age girl's drinking and sex-for-approval would, read alongside his texts, rebut the younger Harrison's phallocentrism.

The introduction of recognizably American speech(es) and diction(s) into formal poetry by writers as disparate as Langston Hughes, Robert Frost, Edna St. Vincent Millay, Robert Hayden, and Gwendolyn Brooks was itself a radical and necessary liberation, still in progress. Tony Harrison's best work exemplifies the power of the specific in poetry, as well as the serviceability of elegant form for everyday use. It makes an "outsider's" language accessible at the same time as its embodiment of the struggle lived through that language makes poetry itself accessible. I hope this book finds a wide American public, particularly among readers whom it will empower, by example, to hear—on the page, too—and to utter, with pen and voice, our own mellifluous and varied mother tongues.

Guy Goffette

Guy Goffette is one of the most unabashedly lyrical contemporary French poets, at a time when, for English language readers at least, contemporary French poetry is characterized, or caricatured, as abstract, more concerned with concepts than with human experience (including history) and feeling: resolutely "difficult." Here is a poet whose work is diffused with humor, longing, tenderness, nostalgia, and occasional cruelty, who does not hesitate to hint, at least, at narrative. He makes use of the quirks of language (follow the sentences and transformations meandering within his parentheses if you can) to mirror the quirks of thought; his deployment of myth is never far from concrete and earthy evocations of childhood, of emotional loss or physical passion.

Guy Goffette was born in Jamoigne, in the Lorraine region, but on the Belgian side of the border, in 1947. This bit of geography has been French and Belgian at different times in its history, and the shifting and permeability of borders has always been primary among the poet's subjects. He lived in northern France for many years, and worked as a bookseller and as a schoolteacher. His austere and prematurely ruptured childhood is eloquently invoked in a book of literary memoir, *Partance et autres lieux*, published in 2000, which also sets forth some keys to his work:

> Once, I dreamed of leaving for the sake of leaving and I always returned. Now I leave without budging, and there is no coming back. You never leave, wrote Rimbaud, which could also be understood as: one never stops leaving, and the real journeys aren't the ones you'd think. That nonexistent sea

beyond the poplars is more real to me than the sea, and far-
ther away than all the Abyssinias. It's enough to let myself go.

(Rimbaud's "On ne part pas" occurs more than once as a reference or an epigraph in Guy Goffette's writings.)

Nonetheless, he has traveled, both near—back and forth between Belgium and France, all through France, and in the
Netherlands—and far, to Greece, to Eastern Europe, to pre-
Katrina Louisiana, on the trail of the blues. Like his friend and
early mentor, the poet Jacques Réda, he is a jazz enthusiast. He
lives now in central Paris, where he works as an editor at Gallimard, and is closely but informally allied with poet-friends of his
generation like Hédi Kaddour and Paul de Roux.

Goffette's voice dialogues with these and lively others in the
landscape of modern and contemporary French poetry (even if
French readers themselves, the cultivated readers who buy the
new Quignard, even the new Cixous, and can catch a quote from
Ronsard or Baudelaire, will all too often say that they know nothing of contemporary poetry, and don't like what they know . . .).
The OuLiPian Jacques Roubaud, who is nonetheless a melancholy chronicler of the changing cityscape and an unforgettable
elegist; the *piéton de Paris* in rhymed verse and in prose, Jacques
Réda; Hédi Kaddour, whose sonnet-like aperçus of contemporary life imply historical narrative behind them; the also-Belgian
William Cliff, one of the few European Francophone *poets* since
Genet to write openly—in rhymed stanzas and sonnets—about
gay sexuality; the much younger Valérie Rouzeau, who marries a
slangy demotic diction to received or metered forms, are a few
of these. Verlaine, the critic Jacques Borel reminds us, was the
poet whom Rilke's Malte Laurids Brigge evoked as his exemplar
of the art—and since Borel wrote this in an essay about Goffette,
we are, and not erroneously, invited to think of Rilke, Verlaine
and Goffette triangulated, and consider what the contemporary
poet Goffette has drawn from these two past poles. If Goffette's
lyrics sometimes partake of a density and simplicity of emotional
thrust combined with prosodic *legerdemain* that is reminiscent of
Verlaine, his attention to the tactile world, to objects as well as
landscape, almost as sculptorly as painterly, connects him with

that master of the quotidian still-life (and of transcendence through the quotidian), Jean Follain, whose work (except for one book of urban prose sketches) also returns almost obsessively to rural landscapes of childhood and youth.

The publication of Goffette's *Éloge pour une cuisine de province* in 1988 brought the poet—already the author of several small-press collections—to the attention of a literary readership accustomed to ignoring poetry. The book's central paradox: the longing of one who muses men were not made, after all, to live in houses, but pause in trees like migratory birds, while chronicling the palimpsests of life within the house's walls, within its kitchened heart; its evocation of the dreams and daring born in northern "villages of dark, cold schist" where a child of ten with "eternity under his cap" waits impatiently to grow up, gave readers some of the satisfactions and recognition they had come to expect only from fiction, while reminding them subtly of poetry's too-long ignored connection with song:

> The art of being born one morning in a provincial kitchen
>   surrounded by jackdaws
> (Oh the gray grief of women underscored by distance)
>
> The art of talking to yourself in a provincial kitchen without
>   expecting an answer
> (The horse whinnies at the field's edge, is death less dense?)
>
> The art of waiting for nightfall in a provincial kitchen
>   undoing stitch by stitch
> the dress of light that clothed my mother and my mother's
>   mother (the cat's eyes assure me it will be my shroud)
>
> The art of making love in a provincial kitchen with words
>   rolled
> in ink and flour—and the woman forever weary like a heart
>   that doesn't reach the margin
>   ("The Art Of")

Goffette's subsequent books of poems explore the themes he set for himself (which seemed, like Proust's opening volume, to contain the possibility of a lifetime's elaborations) while deploying more knowingly, with more of a virtuoso's hand, the possibilities of poetic form and shape (received form, invented form, metrics used in homage, slant and internal rhyme), as the speaker's journey takes him well beyond the poplars at road's edge.

But where did his imagination's journey take him, after all? Paris is more central to French writing, poetry and prose, than any city in the United States has been to American literature. Among contemporary poets for whom landscape, narration, and context are significant, the city *intra muros* figures largely in the work of Raymond Queneau, Michel Deguy, Marie-Claire Bancquart, Franck Venaille, Hédi Kaddour, Jacques Roubaud, and Jacques Réda, to name a few. But Goffette, thoroughly contemporary, aligned to several of these poets in style, and aspiring to the same models (which include Pavese, Hölderlin, Cavafy, Borges, Auden), finds the sources of his work almost entirely in the provinces, not so much in a richness of tradition (barely mentioned) as in a sense of being in a place from which his speaker is perpetually ready to depart. Paris—as a destination or a setting—is barely present. Even the streetcar in the urban/ekphrastic poem from a Lartigue photograph is, in fact, making its way down a New York avenue, not a Hausmannian boulevard. The closest the poems in this collection come to Paris is the evocation of the working-class and immigrant banlieues in the sequence "Cuckoo's Bread," where the Touareg child and the Kabyle merchant in the poem's present, when juxtaposed with the remembered father's vulnerable work-hardened hands, seem to promise to and share with the speaker a depth of (different) memory and a larger horizon.

> What flavor it still keeps here, on my detour
> around the worksite, my father's cuckoo's bread! It's
> like the song of the desert, I imagine, in the voice
> of the young Touareg making the sand fly
>
> from the sandbox in the Cité Victor-Hugo. She has not
> crossed the ocean and knows nothing about simoons,
> but sand, there it is, it's in her, it is her
> and the sea stays below it, in windowpanes, in the eyes
>
> of the old Kabyle in the market: that little patch
> of blue which sparkles, tenderness or what else?
> Perhaps the joy of hearing, evenings, in the suburb,

mixed with swifts' cries, those who are called by,
who answer to, these names of flowers, of wind, of sand:
Hans, Idriss, Tonio, Marjolaine, Sarah.
                    ("Cuckoo's Bread")

One does not "leave" a place behind (physically or in spirit)
without, often enough, leaving people, or a particular person.
The theme of love and rupture, or separation, of desire and de-
tumescence in more than its merely physical aspect, is a constant
presence in Goffette's poems. Perhaps its most striking occurrence in this collection is the sequence "Waiting" ("L'attente") in
which the woman perpetually waiting for her peripatetic lover is
given a voice, wounded, earthy, and powerful:

> If you've come to stay, she says, don't speak.
> The rain and the wind on the roof-tiles are enough
> and the silence piled up on the furniture
> like dust for centuries without you.
>
> Don't speak yet. Listen to what was
> the knife in my flesh: each step, a far-off laugh,
> some mongrel barking, the car door slamming
> and that train which continues to pass and pass
>
> over my bones. Keep still: there's nothing to say.
> Let the rain turn into rain again
> and the wind be that tide beneath the roof-tiles, let
>
> the cur cry his name into the night, the car door
> slam, the stranger leave, in this null place
> where I was dying. Stay if you've come to stay.

—in counterpoint to the disabused libertine voice (in Verlaine's
and Rimbaud's shadow) of the solitary speaker in the Charlestown Blues sequence:

> Curtains, blinds, draperies, shades, no, nothing
> Madame, to conceal from your Cyclops' eye
> in the shadows from which it spies on me
> this long pale body, false corpse tired out
> with debauchery, which is swooning too
> before your balcony, with your drying

> stockings and scanties of a nun at bay—
> poisonous flowers for a lonely man
> whom death panics, draws erect, demarrows
> in the night, riveted to your white thighs.

("Letter to the unknown woman across the street, 1")

The evocation of the erotic in Goffette's work is both discreet and powerful, working through indirection (the view of the ceiling after coitus, the repeated motif of a glimpsed stocking, more evocative than nudity), acknowledging the point of view of the male who sees both promise/redemption and the chill mortal shadow in the act of love and its release, both fantasies less than inclusive of a partner's point of view. (Another poem, a "true" sonnet not yet translated, based on a painting by a contemporary artist, Catherine Lopès-Curval, is in the voice of an abandoned lover who transforms herself into a harpy-like bird of prey and flies off having had her revenge, still wearing lacework stockings.)

Goffette makes frequent homage to his sources, however oblique, in an ongoing series of *Dilectures*—doubled readings of predilection and delectation. *Dilection* is a literary French word for "cherishing," or the love of God for the created world—but there is an undercurrent of misreading, "unreading," "disreading" in the neologism as well. These poems are deft verse portraits of writers as diverse as Auden, Ritsos, Borges, Max Jacob, Valéry Larbaud, Pound, Pavese, Rimbaud, and, of course Verlaine, to whom Goffette also devoted an innovative prose book, neither biography nor criticism but a poet's re-imagination of another poet's life and mind. Goffette claims Verlaine, product of a similar geography, as one of his literary godfathers without any compunction, with no scorn, quite the contrary, for the musicality, eroticism, and nostalgia associated with Verlaine's poetry.

He has written a similar volume on Bonnard, and some of his poetic homages are to visual artists as well—the Symbolist artist Félicien Rops and the photographer Jean-Henri Lartigue; in *Un Manteau de Fortune*, to Catherine Lopès-Curval, above. Auden, that least French of poets and critics, has fascinated Guy Goffette for years, and a recent book, *L'Oeil de la baleine*, addresses him in a equally idiosyncratic prose encounter. The long sequence called "The Raising of Icarus" refers indirectly at once to Auden's poem "Musée des Beaux-Arts" and to the Breughel painting which inspired it.

Despite these homages and acknowledgments of origins, Goffette's is not a "literary," referential poetry, if that means a poetry which requires a gloss or footnotes to be understood; nor is it self-referential as American autobiographical poetry might be taken to be (or the fashionable French "autofiction"). I believe that Guy Goffette's poetry can be enjoyed even by a reader whose ear does not vibrate to the often-present echoes; and the writer or painter subjects of his homages come alive as independent portrait subjects. Whatever echoes he calls forth, Goffette is a poet who makes use (as Paul Claudel, himself the subject of a lengthy "dilecture," proposed in his own *ars poetica*) of quotidian words, everyday expressions, and makes them new (as Ezra Pound, elsewhere "disread," directed), re-invests them with humor, connotation, and emotion, and with a tragicomic festivity. He is also a poet whose work, in subtext, dialogues with the past of French poetry itself, though this dialogue is an undercurrent, never diverting the poem from its primary direction. The bold and witty "Charlestown Blues," for example, written during a residence in Rimbaud's Charleville, makes use of the decasyllabic dixain, which a French reader would associate, not with the Verlaine/Rimbaud duo/duet/duel but with Maurice Scève's mysterious "Délie," published in Lyon in 1544.

As part of this dialogue, Guy Goffette's ludic tug-of-war with the sonnet, which is evident in his three most recent books, is one attraction, for me, to his work, as a poet who, myself, have often handled (or mauled) de- and reconstructed the form. Goffette has written—and continues occasionally to write—wry, contemporary rhymed sonnets in alexandrines. But a thirteen-line poem, as part of a sequence or standing on its own, made up of three usually unrhymed quatrains and a last line which sometimes, though not always, mounts to the classic twelve syllables, has become Goffette's "signature" strophe since his 1991 collection, *La Vie promise*; he has continued to use it in his two subsequent books. A poet whose references and homages attest to a mastery of received forms, he cautions that, in most of his own writing, he "brushes up against classical versification in passing," preferring a studied "limping" to syllabic perfection. He makes playful reference to his own chosen form in the sequence "The Ascent of the Sonnet"—as he does to simile and its inevitability, even to the caesura (which has a more significant place in the alexandrine than it does in English iambic pentameter, precisely because the pentameter is accentual, and the alexandrine syllabic). It shouldn't be necessary to add, though, that "the sonnet" in this sequence is only "the subject" in that Goffette uses it to demonstrate what, in his eyes, any poem exists to accomplish: build a ladder on which the mind can mount to effect a rescue—however temporary, however figurative—from the scaffold of mortality.

Though Guy Goffette is not an Anglicist, he has made known his admiration for English language poetry, for its specificity and concreteness; his admiration for Philip Larkin and for Robert Frost, as well as for Auden: an unlikely trio who share, however, metrical perfect pitch, a disabused vision of humanity, and a sense nonetheless of human depth beneath apparent drabness. Given Goffette's fondness for homages, it is interesting for an American reader (such as myself) to consider in which other English language poets' work, whether or not known to Guy Goffette, there can be found *correspondances* in the Baudelairean sense, and resonances with the poems in this book. The first such poet to come to my mind is James Wright. Both poets (to my mind) share a post-Romantic rather than a post-modernist sensibility. Their sojourns in cities are equally uneasy; the perpetual appeal of an "elsewhere" is ubiquitous, as are the echoes of a dystopic childhood and a certain solitary's pessimism about human nature. Both also draw frequently on an early mastery of classical forms, which remain a referent, often an echo, even in open-form poems. Both of their poetic personae view the act of love and the emotions which lead to it and which it engenders (it doesn't engender anything else in the poems) as inspiration/salvation and as a reminder of impermanence and mortality. But another reference point for an Anglophone might well be the poetry of Seamus Heaney. Among the things Goffette and Heaney share is a solidity of place, and of objects, with an emphasis on the perceived material thing, its implications suggested. For both poets, the return to a Bronze Age (rather than a Golden Age) of childhood is recurrent, called up by *things* and by sensations; both, too, carry on an ongoing dialogue with the sonnet form, sometimes modifying and inflecting it at will. The poem-homages or *dilectures* are also a point in common, prevalent all through both of their work: Cavafy, Auden, and Pavese (at least) have been the subjects of poems by both Goffette and Heaney. The métro sequence in Goffette's "Raising of Icarus" finds an uncanny echo in Heaney's most recent book, where, in a sonnet sequence, a similarly unsettled traveler descends into a Dantesque London Underground.

After a period in which much highly acclaimed French poetry eschewed the concrete, the lyrical, the narrative, and the quotidian, Guy Goffette's poems have found an enthusiastic readership in the last fifteen years. He received the Grand prix de poésie of the Société des gens de lettres in 1999 for the entirety of his work, and, in 2001, the Grand prix de poésie de l'Académie française for *Un manteau de fortune.* His 1988 collection *Éloge pour une cuisine de province,* along with *La vie promise,* were re-issued in Gallimard's popular pocket-format Poésie series in 2000. At once erotic and lyrical, urbane and unabashedly pastoral, of its time and in constant colloquy with a plethora of traditions, his work ought to help widen the dialogue between Anglophone and Francophone poetry beyond the most resolutely "experimental" schools. But Goffette's poetry is not here to be exemplary, and is singularly unfit for a missionary position: it is here as a source of musical pleasure, of memory-seasoned food for thought, as one more irresistible Invitation to the Voyage.

Poetry and Public Mourning

All elegy is public mourning, unless the poem or essay remains in the writer's notebook, unpublished. All elegy makes temporary public figures both of the writer and the subject. Many of the most moving elegies in literary history were written for people of whose lives and works we readers would know nothing except for the existence of the elegy itself. Even elegies for actual public figures—a queen, a dauphin, a general, a religious martyr—often outlive the notoriety and reputations of their subjects, except for readers who are also, by vocation or avocation, historians specializing in the period. The elegiac poet is not so different in the end from the love poet who makes his/her work public:

> So long as men can breathe, or eyes can see
> So long lives this, and this gives life to thee.

—could just as well have ended an elegy, another reason for "Death [to] be not proud." A hundred years after the fact, words are all that remain of the subject and of the poet, whether or not they were both living at the time of the poem's composition. Some of the greatest elegies are in fact declarations of love: I would put Montaigne's essay on friendship, written in memory of Etienne de la Boétie, dead at thirty-two, in this category. One could also put the American poet Donald Hall's elegies for his wife, the American poet Jane Kenyon, in that class. They have in common with Montaigne that the elegized beloved was also a writer and in that sense a public figure, simultaneously the speaking subject of his or her own discourse in the time-out-of-time that is writing. Montaigne made sure of this by publishing La Boétie's sonnets as an appendix within the body of his Essays—

not in the body of the elegiac essay—while Hall's poetry is often read in tandem with Kenyon's by their contemporaries

And yet elegy individualizes its subject, preserves a "personhood," that is apart from the public sphere, is public only in its reminder of how we all mourn and will (if we're lucky) be mourned. The difference that exists between individual elegy (even for a public figure) and "public mourning" seems to me to be a turning away from that memorialization of personhood to exhort the reader or listener to do something besides reflect upon the brevity, the evanescence of life and the existential scandal of death. Donald Hall would like us to read Jane Kenyon's poetry: that would be "doing something," but it does not impose upon us an opinion or a conviction. Is the elegist seeking to depose the tyrant who had her teacher executed? Is the elegist looking to rouse a lynch mob at his sister's funeral? (Montaigne may have wished to deflect attention from the arguably seditious nature of his friend's nonpoetic writings.)

In a Gristede's supermarket a block from my apartment on Manhattan's Upper West Side, the (un-ecological) yellow plastic bags given out to carry purchases are imprinted with a Manhattan skyline silhouette including the World Trade Center towers, and the sentences "We'll always remember," "Always in our hearts," and "Never Forget What They Did." This last sentence perplexes and disturbs me. (It's a constant reminder to bring along the more ecological cloth shopping bag from a local bookstore.) "What They Did"? The dead jihadi kamikazes? What is the purpose of exhorting shoppers to commemorate, specifically, THEIR DEED (not the three thousand plus lives lost, or the widows, widowers, and orphans, or the heroic firefighters, or the amputated skyline) if not an incitement to revenge against "them"? But that particular "they" is nineteen dead men burned to ash. Revenge against whom, then? Osama bin Laden? Whatever target the government provides, as when the majority of Americans came to believe the perpetrators were Iraqis? These words, this bit of advertising, no doubt created out of the belief that New York loyalty and patriotism are good for business, are both a form of public mourning which makes use of words, and an illustration of how readily public mourning can be diverted to other ends. These bags are still given out in 2006, almost five years after the event. Was "Never Forget What They Did" written in Japanese on shopping bags in Hiroshima? Some Americans have selective memories, would like "September 11" to be a world-wide day of mourning, but Hiroshima Day forgotten.

The memory those bags and their text recall to me is of being in a bar near Columbia University on the afternoon of September 11, 2001, watching the reportage on their television—I don't have one. Over and over, almost as frequently as the shots of the explosions, and the dust-white crowd fleeing up the hazy streets, a short film clip was shown of what was said to be Palestinians in a refugee camp exulting at the news: a few men and—mostly—small boys, themselves watching a television set up in an unpaved street, cheering, as for a football game. Behind me, a man who looked like a typical upper West Sider, a.k.a. "a liberal," with a graying blondish beard, in Bermudas, was muttering, "If they did it, Arabs, kill them all!" Why that clip, over and over again—not foreign heads of state expressing sympathy and outrage, reactions in Ohio and Nebraska, Parisians and Muscovites watching the news in disbelief, but a scene without context which seemed to equate those, even children in refugee camps, who were other than appropriately horrified at the disaster with its perpetrators?.

Americans have currently been encouraged, or manipulated, by the current government to mourn on a large public scale, not by writing elegies but by sanctioning or participating in the organized killing, maiming, and despoiling of other people, whether or not those others are at the source of their (manipulated) grief. We (Americans) are hardly the only ones to have put mourning to such use, but we are currently, along with the Israelis, the most notorious globally, which is not to say that Palestinians, Kashmiris, Lebanese, Sudanese, Serbs, Croats, Turks, and Tchetchens (the list is endless, back down the centuries), do not share this propensity. I am not the only American whose almost-immediate reaction to the news of the suicide bombing of the World Trade Center was "What will they do? They'll start a war—any war"—and "they" was not "terrorists." "Terrible things are going to be done in our name," a natural scientist friend said to his poet partner. Our horror and grief at what had happened to fellow New Yorkers and to our city was overcast by fear of a government we did not trust. But we, Americans again, have the circumstances we've been given, since we have not yet found or demanded a way to change them. Under these circumstances, the expression of a certain kind of public mourning, which results in the memorialization, decontextualization, and reification of a tragic event, is, at best, disingenuous.

I think the 250,000 nearly-unnoticed people who arrived in Washington, D.C. in September 2005 to protest the unjust, unnecessary, unsuccessful, and ruinously expensive war in Iraq were joined in—among other things—a communal ceremony of mourning for the American soldiers killed and maimed, and for the thousands more Iraqis killed and maimed, in the ongoing conveniently manufactured conflict: the ceremony of mourning over which this President will not preside. But the American media paid them scant notice, and the Capitol's efficient way of herding demonstrators into a few blocks' circumference prevented them from being seen even by the majority of inhabitants of Washington. Cindy Sheehan and her supporters have been engaging in public mourning, at the encampment in Texas and again in front of the White House. The absence of Ms. Sheehan's name in a discussion of public mourning and its purpose surprises me. She, more than any American writer, has been told to silence her grief by those in power, and been threatened for her expression of it, but her grief has also energized the action of others.

However, and here's the rub: public mourning, whether in the form of poetry or television news clips, risks being used as propaganda; sometimes, indeed, that's its stated intention. Like most of us, I will tend to approve of propaganda for what I already believe / have been convinced to be right; I will wince or rail at the propaganda for what I deplore and contest. Auden wished to excise some of his early political poetry from his oeuvre because he had ceased to hold the convictions there expressed: many readers go on reading these poems, wherever they stand on their politics. His "September 1, 1939," written on the outbreak of World War II in Europe, one of those suppressed poems, was widely circulated on the Internet in the fall of 2001:

> I and the public know
> What all schoolchildren learn:
> Those to whom evil is done
> Do evil in return.

Americans and others read in it a response to what had happened in New York. It seems applicable in 2006 to much of what has transpired subsequently: the American war on Iraq; this summer's war on Lebanese soil between Israel and the Hezbollah, with another twelve hundred dead Lebanese civilians.

I think many poems with a propagandistic agenda transcend it (however worthy or unworthy an agenda it is), and remain good poems when the issue is no longer relevant. But the blurring of elegy and propaganda in poems of public mourning ought at least to be done consciously by the poet: let his or her designs on the reader be honest. That still does not obviate the danger that a piece of elegiac writing not created in the intention of inflaming a spirit of revenge will be used for (or perverted to) that purpose by someone other than the author, a danger Adrienne Rich touches on:

> Poetry never stood a chance
> of standing outside history.
> One line typed twenty years ago
> can be blazed on a wall in spraypaint
> to glorify art as detachment
> or torture of those we
> did not love but also
> did not want to kill
>
> We move but our words stand
> become responsible
> for more than we intended
>
> and this is verbal privilege
> ("North American Time," 1983)

Dylan Thomas's poems "Refusal to Mourn the Death by Fire of a Child in London" and "Among Those Killed in the Dawn Raid Was a Man Aged a Hundred," elegies for victims of the World War II bombing of London, refuse a public stance on anything but the deaths (despite the first title) mourned:

> I shall not murder
> The mankind of her going with a grave truth
> Nor blaspheme down the stations of the breath
> With any further
> Elegy of innocence and youth

We're not being enjoined to hate the Nazis, to support the British war effort, or even (except indirectly) to deplore war waged on civilians, nor are we being enjoined to think of current atrocities as unique in human history. The same can be said of the sections of H.D.'s "The Walls do Not Fall" also written during the Blitz. But what would have been, what would be, the effect of projecting these lines in perpetuity on the reconstructed wall of a bombed building? Would that have been congruent with either poet's project?

The Israeli poet Avot Yeshurun wrote that, if the response to an atrocity is "Never Again," something in the human world may change; if it is "Never Again To Us," the "we" in question and whomever "we" encounter will be doomed to risk, to suffer, and to perpetrate atrocity anew. It seems to me that one potential ethical problem which can arise from a collectively sanctioned public mourning with an official imprimatur is that "Never Again To Us" is the automatic, equally public response. "Never Forget What They Did."

As an American, I would prefer that my taxes which go out in foreign aid not come back into the domestic coffers of what Dwight Eisenhower named "the military-industrial complex" and pay for weapons used to destroy civilian property and kill civilians for whom, given the money trail, it is almost obscene for me to write elegies. (June Jordan's furious 1982, in-your-face poem "An Apology to All the People in Lebanon" could be printed again today.) As a Manhattanite, I would prefer to have seen the World Trade Center site become a medium-rise Jane Jacobs–inspired low-to-middle income housing complex with neighborhood shops, a small park, a playground, a day-care center, a clinic, and a community center where poetry readings, not all elegiac, were among the events on the program. And yes, plaques with poems on the playground walls.

Mortal Moralities

Josephine Jacobsen's The Sisters

The work of Josephine Jacobsen is one of the best-kept secrets of contemporary American literature. She is a coeval of Auden and Roethke, Bishop, Miles and Rukeyser; though a late starter, her first book was published in 1940, her most recent ones this year and last (1986 and 1987). Unlike those others, she is still alive and writing. She shares with Bishop a passion for travel and a sense of being most at home somewhere radically else; with Miles, moral imperatives expressed through the quotidian, the anecdotal; with the later Auden, an aesthetic informed by faith; with Rukeyser, the theme of human interparticipation, the credo *nihil humanum a me alienum est;* with Roethke (and James Wright), the love for the human creature others would find grotesque, merely pitiable, or fatally boring. She was Poetry Consultant to the Library of Congress for six years and is a Fellow of the Academy of American Poets, but her work is not to be found in the Nortons, nor in the proliferation of women's/regional/ aesthetic-affinity anthologies. Five of her six previous books of poetry are out of print. So I greet with great pleasure the appearance of her seventh book of poetry, *The Sisters,* and her second book of short fiction, *Adios, Mr. Moxley.*

Jacobsen is an idiosyncratic, unfashionable, and accessible writer, whose work, neither polemical nor hermetic, eschews irony for the clarity of intelligence and ethical engagement. Her season is spring, her setting as often a hospital (for diseases of the body or the mind) as a beach, a hotel room, or a church: places of passage, providing occasion for communication/ communion, terror, sometimes epiphany. The old, the infirm, the nondescript celibate middle-aged of both genders are often her protagonists, her personae. The young appear at the perilous end of childhood, even in their twenties, with sexual and emotional initiation behind them; moral initiation, at any age, is Jacobsen's more likely focus.

Jacobsen's vision is tragic, and, in both her poetry and fiction, is made manifest most frequently in observations of the quotidian. Comfortable, unexceptionable interiorities are shattered by their intersection with others, with events overdetermined by race and class in ways the privileged sometimes deny. The sins of omission, of inattention, capture this writer's imagination, as do their apposite virtues: paying attention to conscience and the world; active agape, learned when there is time to change, to learn. In the story "Protection," a timid retired white man, puzzling the nature of gratuitous malice with which he has been confronted, inadvertently causes the murder of a black youth by the security guard whose racist assumptions he has challenged. In "The Mango Community," a sabbatical-year white family's dabbling in West Indian revolutionary politics leads to the crippling of their child's black best friend, who cannot choose, as they can, to stay or go, to be or not be involved. In a smaller instance of the same moral failure, in "Season's End" the trust of a likable, gifted Hispanic scholarship student is eroded by his teacher's own momentary lapse of trust; the two lose equally in being lost to each other.

The same cautionary theme is found in the poem "Instances of Communication," where the poet/persona herself, by evasion, generates despair:

> I drove five madwomen down a roar-
>   ing redhot turnpike in a July
> noon; the one behind me had a fur
>   ragged coat gathered about her in
>   that furnace;
> she reached in the horrid insides of a
>   purse and offered me a chocolate,
>   liquid
> and appalling, "Look! Look! A
>   bird!" I cried and flung it over the
>   side,

and munched my empty jaws as she
    turned back, and cried, "How
    good!"
And while the others hummed and
    cursed, and watched simply
    suddenly she put
her lips—behind me—to my ear and
    soft as liquid chocolate came purling
the obscene abuse. "Hush, hush,
    Laura, hush," said the nurse; "the
    nice lady
likes you!" Laura did not believe so,
    and went on slowly, softly, with O
    such misery of hate.

And in lines as pared and paradigmatic as those above are seamlessly, deceptively anecdotal, she describes "The Terrible Naive,"
who:

omnipotently shrewd
will whistle
in mirrors; will wrestle,
but only after

securely lashing
yours wrists with
their tough
vulnerability.

There is an element of sexual conservatism in Jacobsen's stories: unmarried lovers always end up badly, with a fatal flaw to
the relationship laid bare ("The Mango Community," "The Ring
of Kerry," "Motion of the Heart"); the refusal of marriage sig-
nals a refusal of commitment, responsibility. The one homosexual character (in "Motion of the Heart") deceives the young
woman he would marry to "normalize" himself while urging on
her an abortion, which she refuses, along with him, when the
truth is (contrivedly) made known. Still, I have read enough
stories of a man suppressing, then claiming, his gay identity,
thus leaving a shadowy female character for whom no emotions

or consequences are imagined, to find Jacobsen's point of view corrective. And the love of the housekeeper, Shauna, for asthmatic, androgynous Mrs. Adair, in "The Ring of Kerry," dwarfs at a glance the conditional connection of the story's heterosexual pair.

This conservatism, too, must be put in the context of Jacobsen's being a Roman Catholic writer, whose active faith informs her work, whose faith's enactment has provided her with subject matter. The mass is the final "instance of communication," celebrated on the Philadelphia docks in a

> cold great warehouse Sunday still,
> up still cold stairs, along
> a dark dim cold thin hall through a
> brown door into a small square
> room with lit
> peaky candles

and in Jacobsen's beloved Grenada by "The black tall priest / his sash embroidered with nutmeg bursting / through its mace," at a service for the healing of the sick in "The Chosen." His beauty is no more finely observed than the peculiar grace of "The Chosen" themselves:

> The faces, color of cocoa, obsidian, sand,
> of bark, or nutmeg, are turned toward the door:
> the choir, quiet, seethes with intention. Now!
> Between two of the strong, the sick ones creep:
> lame, mostly; enormously tough and fragile,
> like dark, bent-over birds. Some
> spectacular ravages; but sadly, largely
> it turns out, the undramatic wounds of age.
> They are lowered into chairs with dignity.
> A tiny old woman chatters, chatters.

The poem is not describing exotic others (a danger it skirts) but examining the unknowable human contract with the nonhuman:

> The healthy leave first,
> not to hurry the honored, in their slow
> return to familiar sheets. If the terms

of the contract
remain mysterious, it is signed. The chosen
wait in their chairs for those not chosen.

The disabled, the retarded, the mentally and the terminally ill
are frequent characters in Jacobsen's poetry and fiction. Two of
the stories take place in hospitals on the eve of major surgery.
But in "Adios, Mr. Moxley," quotidian connections, from passionate love to intense annoyance, fall away in the face of the
mortal question, while in "Vocation" a woman recognizes and
confronts what is, for Jacobsen, the human nadir: the passion-
less will to cause pain. Jacobsen's hospital is a Flemish painter's
parlor; much is revealed on a small canvas. Mr. Mahoney, who
roams the halls in the poem with his name, is a confused old
man stripped to (but not of) his basic humanity by impending
death:

> Tranquilized, Mr. Mahoney still eludes.
> At 2 A.M. in my dark 283
> the wide door cracks, and sudden and silently
> Mr. Mahoney's nutty face obtrudes.
> It is gently snatched back by someone behind it.
> "That is someone else's room. Yours is this way. . . ."

But Jacobsen writes about death and the knowledge of death
(whence comes one kind of heroism) in many settings: a cock-
tail party, a suburban lane, the bank of a dam:

> We talked of pelota; and how the tendrils of vines
> Curl opposite ways in the opposite hemispheres.
> My cousin was dying. By this I mean
> The rate of his disengagement was rapid.
>   ("I Took My Cousin to Prettyboy Dam")

In both these poems, the speaker is present as observer, her own
life only intersecting with the drama enacted. But she is not a
visitor in Room 283: She knows that she, too, at a less rapid rate
of disengagement, is dying.

The title poem of *The Sisters* invites comparison by name and
subject with several other texts. While gender and the condition

of women as a class are not Jacobsen's primary subjects, they are not refused subjects; nor would Jacobsen refuse to be described as a woman poet, not only in the fact of her gender, but in her cross-generational relationship with a tradition.

"The Sisters" is also the title of an ars poetica by Amy Lowell, imagining, in witty blank verse, visits with Sappho, Barrett Browning, and Dickinson, meditating on the "queerness" of "women who write poetry" and their/our interdependence. Since Lowell, a duality between or within women (in particular, between practicality and imagination, the analytic and the synthetic, sense and sensibility) has so often been the subject of women's poems as to constitute a recognizable theme, a genre like the elegy or the epithalamium. In Elinor Wylie's "Little Eclogue," sisters called Solitude and Loneliness, "One like a moth, the other like a mouse," are divided (with authorial irony) by romantic love. Thirty years later, in "In Mind," Denise Levertov contrasted a woman "smelling of /apples or grass" in a "utopian smock," "kind," who "has / no imagination," with a "turbulent moon-ridden girl / or old woman" "who knows strange songs" but "is not kind."

Jacobsen's "Sisters" are, at first reading, a less-metaphorical, fleshly pair at a Caribbean resort, rendered in five-line stanzas by an observer more neighborly than omniscient. Sister B is "easily pleased"; A is "erratic," given to investigations of the unexpected. "The little group of graves by the Old Men's Home" tempts her back:

> to examine the yellow
> and violet cellophane, the rubber pond-lilies
> floating on dust; the whole glittering heap
> of rainbow mound.

After her burst of energy (we do not read these as young sisters) she falls asleep on the beach, while B swims. But, the observer makes it clear, these sisters "recoil" at the thought of separation. "Before bed, A looked at herself in the mirror, using B's eyes," and, while there is no mention of creator and nurturer, poet and muse, no overt statement that A and B are more than middle-aged spinsters on holiday, I read a synthesis here that could not yet have been made by Wylie or Levertov. The athletic, good-natured B, who exults in sunlight and lobsters, and the mercurial, curious A, whose imagination is awakened and exhausted by death, participate in each other willingly and surely as the nouns "solid as objects" complete the abstract "who, why, go" in poetry as on the sisters' Scrabble board. Woman and poet are not polar; they describe a whole.

For Jacobsen, the aims of a woman's art are those of an art committed to human survival. She is cool toward any art that is not. In "Food," woman's work is the irreducible basis of human possibility:

> To trap, to kill, to drive
> the dogs' ferocity is heroic to tell:
> full-bellied sagas' stuff.
>
> The clawing for heather, the black curved nails,
> cramped breath for smoke, smoke for breath,
> the witch mask clamped on the bride face
>
> bring nothing but life for the nourished.
> . . . .
> By her breath, flesh, her hands, no
> reputation will be made, no
> saga descend. It is only the
>
> next day made possible.

Josephine Jacobsen's writing makes the next day possible.

Hayden Carruth,
American Anarchist

> Where I am is the cosmic individual. Nothing grand,
> nothing romantic. A duck blown out to sea and still
> squawking.
> —"Fragments of an Autobiography"

In many ways, Hayden Carruth is a quintessentially American
poet, his work precisely what an exacting European reader
would expect or wish an American poet to have written. Or at
least, that is my inference as a transatlantic American. Carruth
is rooted in particular American landscapes, specifically Vermont and upstate New York (he was born in Connecticut in
1921) and these locations have not only been central to (and
productive of) his work; they have been the subjects of his most
profound poetic analyses and meditations—as well as the necessary settings of dramatic monologues and narratives. Whereas
Robert Frost gave his readers New England in a kind of fixed,
trans-historical and almost theatrical present (that of the early
twentieth century), Carruth's excavations examine the socio-
political, literary, even geological histories of his locales, and
project them into a very contemporary present and, by inference, into a pessimistically viewed future. The implications of
Carruth's poetry are never limited by a locale: its specificity is its
point of departure for a humanist universality; its accessibility
and its creation of complex personae, engaging or rebarbative,
are the basis for the lyrical complexity of its deployment of
words, syntax, and metrical music.

Though Carruth has never been an urban poet, jazz, that
most urban and American of art forms, informs his work from
myriad directions, whether that be the re-creation of a leg-

endary but historical jam session in 1944 (at which he was not present), a comic-bawdy neo-Greek myth of the newborn Hermes inventing the saxophone in Harlem, or in the application of jazz's techniques of improvisation upon received melodies/ forms to numerous and varied poems. He has been an enthusiastic amateur jazz and classical clarinetist. (*Suicides and Jazzers* is one of his books of critical essays; *Doctor Jazz* is his most recent book of poems, and the title of *Scrambled Eggs and Whiskey,* his 1996 National Book Award–winning collection, refers to a jazz group's five AM breakfast after an all-night set.)

For a variety of reasons, including agoraphobia, Carruth, except for his army stint in World War II, has remained almost consistently in the United States, in his corner of it—unlike his near-contemporaries of the previous decade, Lowell and Bishop, and his coevals James Wright, Carolyn Kizer, Marie Ponsot, W. S. Merwin, and James Merrill, all of whose "cosmopolitanism" counterpoints their American identities (and Bishop's formative universe was Canadian) at many turns. Nor did Carruth emerge from an "Ivy League" university. Yet the polymath breadth and depth of his knowledge, whether it be of prosody, the Napoleonic wars, the techniques of small farming, the influence of the troubadors and the Lingua d'Oc on Western civilization, geology, classical Chinese poetry or, again, jazz, is everywhere evident in his poems and essays, without ever assuming the boys' club preciosity I sometimes associate with Pound or Lowell. Whatever information Carruth imparts is there as the flesh and bones of the poem.

Carruth gives us ample facts about his own life and intellectual history in his poems, and in several of his essay collections, notably *Suicides and Jazzers* and *Reluctantly* (Copper Canyon Press, 1998): from childhood in Connecticut, a journalist grandfather, precocity in a state school accompanied by a creditable performance as an ordinary small boy, to a vivid description of the converted Vermont cowshed that was his studio for decades, his experience of fatherhood, and the explicit details of a 1988 suicide attempt. Yet if the "confessional" school actually existed (a fact I'd question), his work in poetry, at least after the 1950s, is of another vein, in which the individual persona is primarily the vehicle of observation and transformation. The opening of

"Essay on Stone" (1978) is typical of Carruth: the title indicating some exposition, the modified alcaic stanza, the solid location, the gruff and local speaker letting us know quickly enough that there will be a counterpoint between a fixed place and season and the mental traveler's departures:

> April abomination, that's what I call
> this wet snow sneaking down day after day,
>   down the edges of air, when we
>   were primed for spring.
>
> The flowers of May will come next week—in theory.
> and I suppose that witty sentimentalist,
>   Heine, saw the same snow falling
>   in the North Sea

Carruth has always been, among his many other attributes, a "nature poet," that is, a poet who observes the natural world around him keenly, and makes use of that fine observation—which is of the same order as his observation of the interworkings of a jazz quintet, or of a the body of a woman standing in his bedroom's moonlight. He knows the way light in his meadow changes daily with the mutable seasons, the names of its wildflowers, the lives of its trees, as well as the precise actions and physical stresses required to split a cord of wood with an axe—the subject or occasion of several poems. But the observation of nature rendered into a lyric is rarely the goal of his poems. It is the intersection of human consciousness (another aspect of "nature," after all, upon which the idea of "Nature" depends) with tree, stone, rock, river, meadow: the human mind observing its own divagations—whether it's the interrogation of Heine in the poem above, or a reflection on the processes that lead to the beauty, formality, and strangeness of the "natural."

> The snow sculpts this object,
> a snow-tree, and does it
> neither by carving nor
> by molding, for there is
> a third way nature knows
> and a few men besides

          (who will not give themselves
          to the controversies
          of theorists) . . .
     ("Loneliness, an Outburst of Hexasyllabics")

Carruth is one of the most prolific poets of his generation. Writing this, I think of another poet, eight years his senior, Muriel Rukeyser, equally polymath, equally prolific, equally political, and equally out of the "mainstream" critical eye. While they were marked, as is any American poet born after 1910, by the seismic shock of modernism, their work cannot be placed easily either in any of its currents or in the counter-current represented by lyricists like Millay or Randall Jarrell. This may have something to do with the paucity of criticism devoted to their work: in Rukeyser's case, a silence that lasted through the McCarthy era and the ascendance of the New Criticism till the women's movement; in Carruth's case, an inadequacy of response that seems to continue today. Rukeyser was a democratic socialist and urban as Carruth is rural; Carruth, the countryman is a self-proclaimed anarchist. She was an activist and, I believe, an optimist about human possibility. He, prevented by agoraphobia and temperament from extra-literary political action other than sheltering draft resisters in the 1960s, thinks otherwise:

          Now tell me if we don't need a revolution! Black
          is the color of my only flag/
                                   and of man's hope.
          Will revolution bring the farms back?
          Gone, gone. The only crop
          this valley will grow now is the great landwrack,
          breakage, erosion, garbage, trash, gimcrack.
          We burn it. The stink trails in the air . . .
          . . . .
          . . . . his fate
          a need without a hope: the will to resist.
          The State is universal. The Universe is a state.
          Now ask me if I am really an anarchist.

This is from the twenty-second of a series of twenty-eight "Paragraphs" written in the late 1970s (which, I might amend, finishes with the apotheosis of the five-man jazz recording session in 1944 that could be taken to contradict the implications of the above). The "paragraph" is one of Carruth's many prosodic inventions, one of which he has made use frequently over some forty-five years in four significant sequences (to which I'll return).

Carruth is the author of, by my count, twenty-three books of poems (not counting Selected or Collected volumes), a novel, and six collections of essays. These last include a thoroughly idiosyncratic "meditation" on Camus's *The Stranger*, published in 1965, which resembles a contemporary French "autofiction" more than a critical essay, in which a surrogate of the writer interacts with fictional and fictionalized characters—here, Camus himself and characters from Camus's other novels. (Again as a point of reference Rukeyser's books on Wendell Wilkie and the physicist Willard Gibbs: these are two poets for whom encounters, on the page, with minds and ways of thinking different from their own have been essential.)

Carruth is a virtuoso of English prosody and all those metrics and strategies which can be transposed to English. Unlike some of his friends and contemporaries, he does not seem to have had a "conversion experience" moving him from fixed to open forms (I notice now that his compendium collections do not include much work written before his mid-thirties), but he has used both fluently and to the strongest effect from the outset. Furthermore, though he is an accomplished sonneteer and has frequently worked with terza rima, nonce forms, from the simplest to the most complex, have been the instrument and source of much of his strongest work. "Loneliness: An Outburst of Hexasyllabics," quoted above, is an up-country dark night of the soul following the speaker from dusk till dawn in deepest winter in seventy-odd six-syllable lines. I've also mentioned the "paragraph." This is a form Carruth devised in 1957 during internment in a mental hospital, to keep himself sane, one gathers, and the first sequence he produced in the form, on that occasion, is called "The Asylum." The "paragraph" is a fifteen-line poem, which, like a sonnet, can either stand alone or work in sequence. It has a fixed rhyme scheme, and a fixed variation in the number of stresses per line (it is accentual rather than accentual-syllabic, though there is quite a bit of not-necessarily inadvertent iambic pentameter in most of them). With the letter representing rhyme and the numeral the number of stresses, the template would look like this:

> 5A A carpet raveling on the loom a girl
> 5B with a widowspeak and misty legs a moon
> 4A like a fisheye rising from a pool
> 3B a black longwing loon
> 5A bursting afire in the sunset a torn sail
> 5A groveling in a wave a whisper in a stairwell
> 4C a helmet upturned in the black rain
> 4C and later a star reflected on a coin
> 5D glimmering on seastones a sound of motors
> 3E and machineguns
> 5D in the dawn a kiss and candleflame a sonata
> 4E for clarinet a bone cracking a woman
> 5F wearing a blue veil and in Kashan a room
> 5E where the little darkeyed weaving girls lay down
> 5F and died a carpet raveling on a loom.

The poem I've used to illustrate the template is from "Contra Mortem," a sequence of thirty paragraphs written in 1966, in which Carruth "loosened" his own strict form somewhat (one could read lines 8 and 12 as having five stresses) as well as being freer with punctuation, which here follows the trajectory of a free-associative but directed thought-and-image process.

The apotheosis of the paragraph as form and as the fueling energy of a book-length poem came with "The Sleeping Beauty," written between 1970 and 1980 (reissued by Copper Canyon Press in 1990). This 125-poem sequence uses the fairy/folk-tale figure, connected to Carruth initially by the name of his second wife, Rose Marie Dorn (the *Dornröschen,* Briar Rose, is the Sleeping Beauty in German) as a focal point for a meditation on history here not-entirely aleatorically embodied by a series of emblematic "H"-initialed figures including Heraclitus, Hermes, Hector, Hölderlin, Hegel, Hitler—and of course Hayden—all episodes in the Beauty-persona's dream. But there are several other fugal, contrapuntal themes threading the sequence: the narrator's dialogue with a probably-revenant old Vermont farmer named Amos; and a series of monologues in female voices—Lilith; a foot-bound Chinese lady of sixteen; a Puritan poet whose husband burns her writings; Bessie Smith. *The Sleeping Beauty* is in fact also a profound consideration of gender and its permutations, its wounds, in each human being (in particular in the Jungian sense of anima/animus, response of and to the "opposite" within each of us, whatever our sexuality). It is perhaps not accidental that the sequence was written during the rise of the "second wave" of the American and British feminist movement (feminist poets Carolyn Kizer and Adrienne Rich are among Carruth's oldest friends). Yet I have never seen it analyzed in that context: a male poet's response to and attempt to integrate the damages of gender polarity—except by Kizer, who wrote of it, upon its publication in 1982, "Those two great contemporary issues, recognition of women and respect for our fragile world, are bound together in profound unity."

Another of Carruth's tours de force is the eminently readable *Asphalt Georgics* (New Directions, 1985). These are poems about the lower-middle-class white inhabitants of the prefabricated towns clustered around strip malls in upstate New York, largely dramatic monologues. Again Carruth invents a form: in this case quatrains of alternating eight and six-syllable lines, with the second and fourth rhyming, often deliberately using hyphenations in the rhyme lines. At times the poet-persona intervenes; in the opening, longest "Georgic," "Names," there's a constant metamorphosis. A husband driving to the mall,

> Friendly and Ponderosa
> looked o.k., but Carvel
> was dilapidated, and Mis-
> ter Donut had a hell
>
> of a big jagged hole through both
> sides of its glass sign. I
> saw the killdeer running that has
> her nest next to the high
>
> way on the gravel strip . . .

is eventually a political prisoner caged in a steel box in Latin America:

My name was Julio. But now
  by enormous effort
I have transformed my consciousness
  to the gleam of consort-

ed light that scintillates round the
  dome of gold on the ca-
thedral all day at the top of
  the capital plaza.

My name is Santa Julia.
  his/her out-of the-body state
. . . attainable by
  all those who must forget

themselves completely and absolutely in order to
pass through and beyond the pain that
  surpasses knowing . . .

In "Marge," Carruth makes a different kind of audacious narrative move. In this monologue, an isolated sixty-year-old recovering alcoholic recounts the story of a lively friendship between the speaker and an older woman, his "landlady," whose death at eighty-five has left him desolate and destitute. But the woman, from her name, and the account of her illness and death, is Carruth's mother (her own life and prolonged death elegized in a long poem written in 1981) who died when the poet was himself sixty. The details of "Charlie Spaid's" drying out are congruent with Carruth's, though the rest of the persona's life is presumably invented. Does the poem incorporate Margery Carruth's death in a fiction, or posthumously bestow upon her a fifteen-year quotidian companionship, never qualified as filial? The poem, like Carruth's Camus book, skates on the edge of two different modes of narrative, and is the more effective for it; it is also a hub around which the created community of the "Georgics" revolves. It's evident that in Carruth's poems, the "local" is never merely parochial, and the personal may be either or at once political, fictional and universal.

Carruth has published two new collections since the *Collected Shorter* and *Collected Longer Poems* of 1992 and 1994: *Scrambled Eggs and Whiskey* (1996) and *Doctor Jazz* (2001), whose appearance marked his eightieth birthday. Carruth has explored innumerable modes and forms in his career, and these books pursue many of them—historical permutations (Timor the Lame; Waterloo), erotic lyrics to his wife, new paragraphs, a memorial poem for the clarinetist-saxophonist Sidney Bechet. Central to the last book is a sixteen-page elegy for Carruth's daughter Martha, dead of liver cancer in her forties, This seems, at first approach, like an expression of unmediated grief and fury, the almost unapproachable raging of a contemporary Lear. But it is no more unmediated than (as much *written* as) Lear's soliloquies, or than the existential solos of Coltrane or Charlie Parker, whose artistry and discipline is such that it informs and forms any "free flight" under the pressure of extremity.

Carruth has had lengthy and fruitful relationships with two editors, unusual in these days of corporate editorial anonymity: James Laughlin of New Directions, upon the occasion of whose death Carruth wrote a book-length memoir-tribute, and Sam Hamill of Copper Canyon Press. The two were or are poet-editors; Hamill is, as well, a scholar and translator of Chinese poetry. Carruth has frequently held dialogue with other writers in his poems: Heine, Ovid, Paul Goodman, Camus, Levertov, Laughlin himself. A new mode in this dialogue perhaps comes to Carruth via Hamill: two sequences that engage classical Chinese poets, "A Summer with Tu Fu" and "Bashö." As in all his interrogations of other aesthetics, Carruth grounds his persona firmly in his own landscape and particularities—which bear a certain relationship to those of the exiled Tu Fu, in the sixth century, and the eccentric haiku master Bashö in the seventeenth, The Bashö sequence is cemented by quizzical haiku:

> After the setbacks
> of Chicago and New York,
> he went to Vermont
>
> to a cowshed nine
> feet square. Was he proud to
> learn that Chomei's hut
>
> in the mountains near
> Kyoto had been "ten feet
> square"? Maybe. Who knows.
> ("The Matter of Huts")

Carruth in his curmudgeon persona grouses or exults that, at eighty, he has another fifteen-hundred-year poetic tradition about which to learn—in which he is already immersed and engaged.

The Sonnet

What does the sonnet do (for the contemporary Anglophone writer)—that it is so persistently attractive, yet so frequently reviled? It would probably surprise a French reader/scholar of contemporary poetry to note how many twentieth-century English language writers have written sonnets and continue to include them in their oeuvre: not only persistent "formalists," from Frost to Auden to Merrill, but poetic iconoclasts like the Americans Jack Spicer, Hayden Carruth, James Wright, and June Jordan and the British Geoffrey Hill; Irish poets like Heaney, Muldoon, and Derek Mahon, British poets Carol Rumens and Glyn Maxwell, Anglophone poets of other origins like the Indians Dom Moraes and Reetika Vazirani, Aga Shahid Ali from Kashmir, the Hungarian George Szirtes, and the Iranian Mimi Khalvati. Yet American student readers, if they are at all a representative example, tend to come to the sonnet with prejudices entirely disproportionate to their very limited experience. The average American college senior, it seems, has read two or three of Shakespeare's sonnets, with very little literary or historical context—no Spenser, Sidney, Lady Mary Wroth, Donne, Milton, Keats, Wordsworth, Barrett Browning, Rossetti, Meredith, Hopkins, Millay, Frost—and yet "knows" that the sonnet is constricting, "difficult" (but trivial), artificial, archaic, etc. (Unfortunately, the majority of American readers of poetry *do* first encounter it in a classroom, rather than on family bookshelves or while browsing in a bookshop or a public library.)

One of the virtues of the American (and increasingly, Anglophone in general) institution of "creative writing" classes is that, as with other forms and freedoms, students reading canonical and contemporary sonnets in the perspective of attempting one themselves discover, along with the pitfalls, the possibilities and challenges opened in the fourteen-line labyrinth. For every re-calcitrant student, there are two who, having composed an initial sonnet, write a sequence of linked ones, and who go back to their literary anthologies and textbooks and discover the above-mentioned writers with the special interest of connoisseurs, appreciating the process as well as the product. One student said, of his first attempt at writing a sonnet, that it was like moving into a new, small-seeming room, and discovering that there was nonetheless room for all of his furniture. (Or, one decides ruthlessly what furnishings are disposable. Or one acquires or constructs new furniture for the room.) Students' reactions to the sonnet seem emblematic of those of contemporary readers: it's a form which invites close engagement, and that engagement often becomes a kind of dialogue with its past and present uses and connotations.

In a contentious part of that dialogue, the sonnet remains the chosen scapegoat for every tirade against the supposed limitations/artificiality/entrammeling of the free spirit imputed to "formal verse," every declaration of its irrelevance and nocive qualities to the literary expression of African Americans, feminists, the progressive working class, the postmodern sensibility, from Pound to Leroi Jones / Amiri Baraka, Adrienne Rich, and Diane Wakoski—who once equated sonnet-writing with fascist politics(!)—and, no doubt, the latest manifestoes. Still, Pound, like every apprentice poet of his generation, wrote countless sonnets including the beautiful and much-anthologized "A Virginal," from his 1912 pamphlet *Riposte*. H.D., a modernist's modernist, for whose early work the rubric of "Imagism" was conceived, atypically prefaced her mid-career volume *Red Roses for Bronze* (1930), with a sonnet, dedicated to her life-companion Winifred Bryher. Gwendolyn Brooks in her first book, *A Street in Bronzeville*, published in 1944, elegantly and economically depicted, in a sonnet sequence of dramatic monologues, the situation of black soldiers returning from World War II to quotidian American racism and segregation.

The sonnet has perhaps the most polyglot and varied history of any European poetic form. It has at different times represented: the claims of popular language over learned Latin; the aspirations of an intellectual or artistic meritocracy in a world of inherited power; idealized love implicitly contrasted with arranged, dynastic marriages; the ambitions of aristocrats; women's longing for autonomy; the soul's struggle with faith and fear of death. The sonnet's invention is credited to a poet called Jacopo (or Giacomo) da Lentini, in Sicily in the early thirteenth century, who developed the fourteen-line model we know from a generalized lyric in "popular" language (Italian; not Latin: *sonetto* = little sound) by combining two Sicilian quatrains—rhyming *abababab*—with a sestet rhymed *cdecde*. This rhyme scheme varied until the adoption and use (first by Guittone d'Arezzo; then indelibly by Petrarch in the fourteenth century) of the double envelope quatrain on two rhymes (*abbaabba*) followed by a sestet (the last six lines) using two or three rhymes in a varied pattern: (*cdecde, cdeedc, ccddee* are three possibilities). The Italian sonnet was written in hendecasyllabic verse: lines of eleven syllables, not regularly stressed (accentual) as is English iambic pentameter (or as Latin verse was) so that the presence of rhyme was necessary to mark the form and turnings of the poem. Simply by looking at these rhyme schemes, the reader sees that all these versions of the sonnet almost predicate a poem whose "argument" divides into two parts, a premise set out in the octave (first eight lines), with the sestet contradicting it, modifying it, or giving a concrete proof. The form also easily incorporates the "If . . . / Then" structure of a mathematical proof. The poet-scholar Paul Oppenheimer argues persuasively that, as well as a lyric in vernacular language, the sonnet represented and heralded a European lyric poetry meant to be read silently rather than sung or performed. While the argument or syllogism described by the structure can approximate a dialogue, it also echoes at least one frequent pattern of silent thought, sweet or not, in what Oppenheimer describes as a "promotion of reason with its resolution of emotional conflicts, one outcome of its severity of structure."

Some feminist critics have claimed that the sonnet, suggesting as it does, in the Petrarchan model, a male poet addressing a distant, idealized and, above all, silent woman, is the *nec plus ultra* of poetic form negating the female subject. But women poets' use of the sonnet goes virtually back to its origins. One of the first women poets (samples of whose work we have extant) to write in a modern European language was "La Compiuta Donzella"—a pseudonym meaning "the accomplished" or "learned maiden." She lived in Florence in the second half of the thirteenth century, predating Dante and Petrarch, and wrote, among other poems, sonnets, three of which survive, only some twenty years after the form had been fixed. And the subject of her sonnets? Not a lover, unattainable or otherwise, but her desire to escape from a marriage arranged by her father and enter a convent—which reminds this reader of another sometime-sonneteer, the Mexican poet Sor Juana Inés de la Cruz, who, four hundred years later, took the veil in order to pursue her real vocation of writing and study. (When the sonnet was introduced in France in the mid-sixteenth century, it was quickly taken up by the entirely nonmonastic Louise Labé.)

More than with any other lyric form, the writer of one sonnet often goes on to a second, connected one, and then to a third or a hundredth: this was true of Petrarch, Shakespeare, Millay, and is true today of Seamus Heaney, Marie Ponsot, or Marilyn Nelson. (This seems less self-evident when one thinks of the paucity of sequences of villanelles or sestinas.) The sonnet is more direct, less "tricky" than other forms inherited by English from Romance languages: it does not require repeated words or lines. Its Italian form is very like a mixture of the two most flexible and utilitarian "blocks" of verse narrative: the quatrain and terza rima. At the same time, the separation of discrete poems in the sequence deflects one's expectation of narrative, permits cinematic shifts in time, place, point of view. There is a paradox in the sonnet sequence, in the act of starting a second sonnet on completing the first: the fourteen-line poem whose initial attraction includes the imminent necessity of closure also proves to be open-ended. Re-writing the last line of a just-completed sonnet to start a new one (and commence a crown) is a prime example of that paradox. Contemporary crowns of sonnets have been written by Marie Ponsot, George Szirtes, Marilyn Nelson, Alberto Ríos, George Macbeth, J. D. McClatchy, Robyn Selman, Mimi Khalvati: the last four have written "heroic" crowns of fifteen sonnets in which the last (or first) poem is made up of the first lines of the fourteen others. But sequences prolong themselves without repeated lines. Edna St. Vincent Millay's "Sonnets from an Ungrafted Tree" is a stark New England narrative about a farm wife. The British poet Tony Harrison's cycle of sixteen-line Meredithian sonnets, a meditation on class and language, becomes an elegy to his working-class father. Cuban American physician-poet Rafael Campo uses the same form to write about family and ethnic culture—and about love between men, and community medicine, in sixteen-sonnet *canciones*.

The sonnet, and the sonnet sequence in particular, also exercise an influence on poems not specifically composed within their formal strictures. Robert Lowell wrote much rhymed and metered formal verse, but there's also no question that the unrhymed blank verse fourteen-line sections of *History, For Lizzie and Harriet*, and *The Dolphin* are profoundly informed by the English sonnet sequence, and are unavoidably read in the light of that tradition. John Berryman and Hayden Carruth, consummate sonneteers, each devised a "nonce" form (Berryman's "Dream Song" eighteen-liners; Carruth's fifteen-line "Paragraph") that departs from the sonnet in metric stricture and yet functions in a way not dissimilar both in isolation and in sequence. Adrienne Rich developed her youthful poetic strength in the exercise of traditional English prosody, which she rejected in the late 1960s as incompatible with progressive, populist, and feminist political engagement. Still, the shadow of the sonnet sequence informs important poems at every stage of her career, "Snapshots of a Daughter-in-Law" and "Twenty-One Love Poems" being among the most significant. Robert Duncan used "Sonnet" as a title for open-form evocations of an incorporeal beloved who may represent the art itself. Ted Berrigan wrote a book-length sequence called "Sonnets," and Bernadette Mayer also uses the genre-name: these are "avant-garde" poets of the New York School who do not, in general, have much truck with fixed forms. Perhaps it is precisely because of modernism's critical resistance to the sonnet that contemporary poets have reexamined it and "made it new" with heterodox content and language at once demotic and experimental. And this (paradoxically) is congruent with its origins: a poem in "popular" language which could be read or written by anyone (not only clerics and scholars) which incited its writers to fresh examination of their evolving languages' interactions with the human world.

As a practitioner of the form, I can attest that one sonnet often leads to another related one, even when that was not the original intention, which also implies the lyric impulse leading to or coexisting with the narrative or meditative one. Indeed, the sonnet sequence seems to combine the virtues of the long—narrative or meditative—poem with those of the short lyric. It eliminates the necessity for the "connective" and explicatory passages which are the bane of writers of narrative verse: in sequence, the individual sonnet can function like a single picture in a series (think of Monet painting the same cathedral at different hours of the day), creating its own implicit connections. In more contemplative or philosophical sequences, it permits, almost requires, a short but meticulous examination of different aspects of the subject under consideration, regarded from different perspectives and distances. Donne's "Holy Sonnets" and "La Corona" are prime canonical examples of this "hologrammatic" quality of the form when used sequentially, as is the group by Hopkins, on a more devastating crisis of faith, often called the "Terrible Sonnets." Auden's sequence, "The Quest," has a similar movement, but also could be compared to a series of exemplary woodcut engravings, or the flat and brilliant progression of scenes in a hagiography rendered with comic-strip precision across the bottom of a quattrocento altarpiece. In narrative sonnet sequences, the individual sonnet often functions like a cinematic "take," zooming in at the necessary moment, then, blackout, new scene on the screen: establishing settings, ideas, and, even or especially, characters and their relationships, by the accumulation of disparate incidents and details. At least this was how I felt it functioned in the composition of my own most ambitious sonnet narrative *Love, Death and the Changing of the Seasons*.

I've chosen to approach the "contemporary sonnet" in an admittedly partisan fashion, by examining sonnets by four poets, three American and one British, who share an allegiance to poetry's, and to the sonnet's, ability to bring into literary discourse voices and vocabularies previously excluded or unexamined. Gwendolyn Brooks and Muriel Rukeyser are coeval with Elizabeth Bishop and May Swenson—a notable generational richness. All four of these women had a volatile relationship with modernism, which was establishing its hegemony over American poetry as they approached maturity as writers. At that time, for both Brooks and Rukeyser, the opposition of accentual verse to open-metered verse was not a subject for polemic: they mastered and practiced the varied forms their craft could take in order to more freely enlarge the scope of what poetry could envision. Their very different uses of the sonnet, linguistically and formally, as well as in their approach to "narrative," also illustrate some strategies important to today's practitioners.

The Rites for Cousin Vit

Carried her unprotesting out the door
Kicked back the casket-stand. But it can't hold her,
That stuff and satin aiming to enfold her,
The lid's contrition nor the bolts before.
Oh oh. Too much. Too much. Even now, surmise,
She rises in the sunshine. There she goes
Back to the bars she knew and the repose
In love-rooms and the things in people's eyes.
Too vital and too squeaking. Must emerge.
Even now, she does the snake-hips with a hiss,
Slaps the bad wine across her shantung, talks
Of pregnancy, guitars and bridgework, walks
In parks or alleys, comes haply on the verge
Of happiness, haply hysterics. Is.

(Gwendolyn Brooks, from *Annie Allen*, 1950)

This sonnet is from Gwendolyn Brooks's *Annie Allen*, the first book by an African American to receive the Pulitzer Prize for poetry. Brooks, born in 1917 in Kansas but a Chicagoan since infancy, is a poet whose strongest work combines contemporary (though rarely demotic) diction with a love of wordplay and supple, elaborate syntax recalling Donne or even Crashaw (and frequently Eliot) which she brings to bear, with affectionate irony, on her subject. *Annie Allen* is a collection of poems which, taken together, chronicle and counterpoint the life of a young woman and of her community: a black working-class neighborhood in Chicago during and just after World War II. That community, and its subsequent transformations, from working-class aspiration to urban decay to the radicalized youth movement of the sixties, remained Brooks's major focus through later books. Throughout a half-century in which an autobiographical aspect has been predominant in American poetry, even in the discretion of Elizabeth Bishop or the verbal legerdemain of cummings, Brooks has constantly eschewed this vein: even in poems spoken in the first person, there are indications that we are reading a dramatic monologue. One could say that the protagonist of each book, and of the work as a whole, is not an individual but a community.

The movement of *Annie Allen* is that of the character, Annie's moving out of romantic self-absorption, and beginning to observe that community—which, for her as for Gwendolyn Brooks, is not limiting, but a source of energy, information, support, and, most of all, of *stories* implicit in the quotidian lives of its citizens. "The Rites for Cousin Vit" is an elegy as well as a sonnet, but it is an elegy so overflowing with the life-force of its subject that, with no overt religious context, it constitutes a denial of death. Although subordinated to the imperative "surmise" which makes this rising an act of imagination, the verbs "rises in sunshine" and "must emerge" metaphorically equate the sensual, down-to-earth Vit with the risen Christ—who then "does the snake-hips with a hiss," becoming both Eve and the serpent, until, after the communion of the "bad wine" and the purely human interaction of "talks," these transcendental identities are resolved with the final verb, a one-syllable sentence of affirmation: "Is." All this is contained—or rather, turned loose—in an Italian sonnet of two envelope quatrains and a sestet framed by the end-words "emerge" and "is." Nothing is accidental here, certainly not the title, in which Vit's name echoes the Latin for "life"—and her identification as "cousin" implicitly creates a narrator/speaker with a familial relationship to her. It also claims her as a community and family member, a fact which informs the "outlaw" aspects of her behavior: the plural "love-rooms," the bad wine, shiny dresses, and dirty dancing. "Outlaw" perhaps, but not outcast.

II

They came to me and said "There is a child."
Fountains of images broke through my land
My swords, my fountains spouted past my eyes
And in my flesh at last I saw. . . . Returned
To where we drove in the high forest, and earth
Turned to glass in the sunset where the wild
Trees struck their roots as deep and visible
As their high branches, the double planted world.

"There is no father," they came and said to me.
I have known fatherless children, the searching, walk
The world, look at all faces for their father's life
Their choice is death or the world. And they do choose.
Earn their brave set of bone, the seeking marvelous look
Of those who lose and use and know their lives.

IV

Now the ideas all change to animals
Loping and gay, now all the images
Transform to leaves, now all these screens of leaves
Are flowing into rivers. I am in love
With rivers, these changing waters carry voices,
Carry all children; carry all delight.
The water-soothed winds move warm above these waves.
The child changes and moves among these waves.

The waves are changing, they tremble from waves of waters
To other essentials—they become waves of light
And wander through my sleep and through my waking,
And through my hands and over my lips and over
Me; brilliant and transformed and clear,
The pure light. Now I am light and nothing more.

(Muriel Rukeyser, *The Green Wave*, 1948)

Muriel Rukeyser, born in Manhattan in 1913, the daughter of middle-class Jews—a cement-manufacture and a bookkeeper—describes herself, in another poem, as having been "born in the first century of world wars." She came to consciousness during World War I; she was seven when American women obtained the right to vote. The trial in 1927 of the immigrant anarchists

Sacco and Vanzetti for treason, and their subsequent execution, shocked and moved her, and awakened in her a life-long political consciousness. "Not Sappho, Sacco," she writes, of her own inspiration, in "Poem Out of Childhood"—an inspiration which led her to include in a book-length poem the testimony she gathered from strip-miners stricken with brown-lung in West Virginia, to go to Spain as a journalist during the civil war in 1936, to protest on-site the imprisonment of a dissident South Korean poet in 1975 when she herself was physically enfeebled by diabetes and a stroke.

The sonnet sequence "Nine Poems for the Unborn Child" was written during Rukeyser's pregnancy in 1947. She was unmarried, and never named her son's father. As far as I know, this sequence is the first to claim for this situation, or multiple situations (the physical and mental stages and changes of pregnancy; a single woman's decision to bear and raise a child) the stature of poetic subject matter, neither melodramatized, stigmatized, nor sentimentalized—at a time when a pregnant single woman character in a play, novel, or film could routinely be expected to miscarry, die, or both. (There's an unmarried mother who doesn't die in Elizabeth Barrett Browning's verse novel *Aurora Leigh,* but she remains an emblematic and redeemed "ruined maiden," not the protagonist.)

1947: the war, Hiroshima, the Shoah, were as present in Rukeyser's worldview as were the events in her own body, and the Cold War was freezing in on American progressive activists. "Nine Poems" is not a minimalist or domesticated sequence, turning away toward the private life in defeat, despair, or resignation. Rather, the sequence posits gestation and birth as a hopeful, chosen antidote to war and to stultifying public and private silences, in which the conscious woman's mind and body also signify the body politic.

Rukeyser never indicated why she chose the sonnet sequence to develop this particular poem. The correspondence of the nine months of pregnancy as discrete "stages" with the connected but separate poems of the sequence, the poet's desire to circumnavigate the subject while avoiding linear movement, and, in her own dialogue with the sonnet form, her desire to inscribe a woman's feelings for her unborn child into the tradition of "praise of an ideal but distant beloved" which has informed the sonnet sequence since Petrarch, may all have contributed to her choice.

"Nine Poems" is a sequence in which the sonnet's lyrical and narrative (indeed, cinematic) possibilities are inflected through Rukeyser's Whitmanian prosodic largesse. Architectures and landscapes, human and animal bodies, furniture, weather, permeate each other, just as pregnancy itself is at once a state of intense interiority and of engagement in human interdependence. Dichotomies are dismantled: the pregnant poet's body is transformed to "pure light," but darkness is also "promise," the place or state where a new kind of vision becomes possible, as the poet is able to "trust in the rhythms of experience" (as she states in her critical book, *The Life of Poetry*). Incorporeal ideas become "animals" (reminding the literal-minded reader of the old "rabbit test" for pregnancy, in which the animal's death indicated the presence of new life).

These are unconventional sonnets—unlike the one of Rukeyser's which is most frequently anthologized, a perfectly rhymed and metered Italian sonnet standing in the midst of "Letter to the Front," a long sequence of wartime poems in various received and open forms which begins "To be a Jew in the 20th century." In the "Unborn Child" sequence, assonance, consonance, and repetition often stand in for rhyme (it is in part the expectations of the sonnet form which encourage the reader to *hear* rhyme echoes in "child/eyes" "land/returned" "wild/world") and the normative iambic pentameter line often swells to twelve or thirteen syllables, and, more iconoclastically, to six or more stresses. Brooks's sonnet, not atypical of her work, never strays from its immediate subject, Vit, and its larger subject, the community, the city, to which Vit returns, "resurrected." Rukeyser's sonnets are at once located within the body of the pregnant speaker and completely uncontained. The "swords" and "fountains" are both within and outside the body; the "waves" are at once water and light, the interpenetration of body and mind, of maternal and fetal consciousness, and the transformative power of some outside, benevolent force. The situational grounding is that of the single woman learning of and welcoming her pregnancy (embracing, like Vit, an "outlaw" status), but this is essentially a point of departure.

The British poet Tony Harrison, while a consummate pro-sodic craftsman who does not, as far as I know, use open forms at all, still carries on an extremely contentious dialogue with the canon of English poetry in general, and with the sonnet in particular, in his ongoing sequence *The School of Eloquence.* Harrison was born in Leeds in 1937 to working-class parents, who spoke in the strongly marked dialect of the province. A "scholarship boy," he received a classical education: from childhood, his experience of the English language was divided between how he spoke at home, and the speech impressed upon him by the academy. He is a gifted linguist who has translated the *Oresteia* and revived the British tradition of verse drama for radio broadcast. But the central subject of his own poems has always been precisely the conflict, within himself and demonstrated historically, between the language of "educated men" and that of the working classes; between the "Received Pronunciation" of the grammar school and the Leeds *patois* of his family. If there is a Laura to Harrison's Petrarch, it is his father, who (like Laura) dies in the course of the sequence, but continues to be addressed as arbiter of the work's worth. But their separation comes, more than from any distance in affection, from the distance created between them by the son's acquisition of standard and literary English. While the foreground is this individual instance of the separations and *rapprochements* created by language, Harrison's larger canvas depicts the way language has historically been used to give voice to some and silence others; how its acquisition has represented empowerment for the working class century after century; but how the loss of the working-class mother tongue also represents a loss of history and connection. While some other English poets of his generation of working-class and provincial origin attempted to create a British equivalent of the American Beat and Black Mountain movements, Harrison has chosen to have it out with the Received Language on its own terrain.

On Not Being Milton

Read and committed to the flames, I call
these sixteen lines that go back to my roots
my Cahier d'un retour au pays natal,
my growing black enough to fit my boots.

The stutter of the scold out of the branks
of condescension, class and counter-class
thickens with glottals to a lumpen mass
of Ludding morphemes closing up their ranks.
Each swung cast-iron Enoch of Leeds stress
clangs a forged music on the frames of Art,
the looms of owned language smashed apart!

Three cheers for mute ingloriousness!

Articulation is the tongue-tied's fighting.
In the silence round all poetry we quote
Tidd the Cato Street conspirator who wrote:

Sir, I Ham a very Bad Hand at Righting.

Continuous

James Cagney was the one up both our streets
His was the only art we ever shared.
A gangster film and a choc ice were the treats
that showed about as much love as he dared.

He'd be my own age now in '49!
The hand that glinted with the ring he wore,
his father's, tipped the cold bar into mine
just as the organist dropped through the floor.

He's on the platform lowered out of sight
to organ music, this time on looped tape,
into a furnace with a blinding light
where only his father's ring will keep its shape

I wear it now to Cagneys on my own
and sense my father's hands cupped round my treat—

they feel as they've been chilled to the bone
from holding my ice cream all through *White Heat.*
(Tony Harrison, from *The School of Eloquence*)

Harrison chose a sixteen-line Meredithian sonnet for his sequence, parts of which have appeared in several of his books,
and which he seems to be continuing: seventy-six were included
in his 1984 *Selected Poems.* "On Not Being Milton," which opens
The School of Eloquence, makes the poet's preoccupations clear: a

return, in the art vouchsafed him by his education, to his origins, in particular to his linguistic sources in demotic speech; against the backdrop of British working-class history. (An "Enoch" was an iron sledgehammer used by the Luddites to smash the metal loom-frames, both made by one Enoch Taylor.) His sonnet-homage to the cinema is one of many by various poets acknowledging the affinities between *le septième art* and the workings of memory from which the lyric springs. (Rukeyser had already written about the film/poetry affinity in *The Life of Poetry* in 1944.) In other sonnets, Harrison incorporates his parents' and childhood friends' Leeds dialect. The poet as a boy ruefully tells his mates why he can't go *off laikin* with them: *Ah bloody can't ah've gorra Latin prose,* in impeccable iambic pentameter—a meter into which dialect English falls as easily as the literary language, Harrison elsewhere points out. Like Muriel Rukeyser's (and like most sonnet sequences) Harrison's poems move back and forth from their source in an individual (we can here assume autobiographical) drama to consideration of a more universally applicable dilemma. Like Gwendolyn Brooks, though, his work attains its "universal" dimension precisely by the degree of specificity it achieves in the evocation of its *dramatis personae* and milieu. Both poets engage their readers, not by assuming that the experiences, settings, or even language evoked, are common to those readers as well, but by making an identification possible through the precision of that evocation, even given the ironic distance that both of them frequently employ,

Marilyn Nelson, born in 1946, author of ten books, came of age as a poet at a time when there was strong pressure on a young African American writer to reject any use of *or* dialogue with received forms, and to create out of a communal and specifically virile rage. Even Gwendolyn Brooks, a poet established both within and outside the black community, whose entire oeuvre chronicled the life of Chicago's South Side from World War II on, proclaimed auto-critically that her engagement with form and vocabulary had distanced her work from that community of origin, and the revolutionary potential of its youth. But for Nelson the complexity of Brooks's narratives, the richness of her language, illustrated precisely a way African American voices, and their way with words inflected, as black English is, with Elizabethan playfulness and Miltonic measure, entered into the discourse of American verse.

Nelson has written eloquently of her own relationship, as an African American poet, with the English canon and with the counter-tradition of the sixties' Black Arts movement. Nelson could, herself, feel the impulse which led Amiri Baraka and others to attempt, instead of that dialectic of inclusion, the creation of a separatist Black Aesthetic. And yet, as she asks herself in her essay, "How can a poet survive such a radical self-amputation?" Like Brooks, her own choice has been the self-reflectiveness of double vision, at once within and outside literary tradition, which establishes a decolonizing dialogue with the canon.

I Sermon in the Cotton Field
Philippians 2:12b–15a

His heart's upswelling of its own accord
slackens the reins, stopping the plow mid-row
beside a sea of furrows, as the word
whirling within takes shape: Whoa, brothers, whoa.
One mule cranes questioningly; the other nips
his neck, ears back. They bray against the hitch
which matches them. And Uncle Warren wraps
his arms around the sky and starts to preach.

Beloved, stop your grumbling. Be the stars
what give a twisted generation light.
That's what the book say. But old Satan roars
louder, sometimes, than Master. He say, Hate
the whip-hand and the yoke: Why be a fool?
The Lord hisself were tempted, Brother Mule.

V Palm Sunday 1866
Peter 2:22–24

Make our hosannas incense on the wind:
may we wave palms of welcome. . . . Listening
from the colored pew, Aunt Sally nods amen.
From beside her, T.T., bored and fidgeting
chases his rubber ball into the aisle.

The front pew kneels at the communion rail,
head bowed. Aunt Sally, reaching for the child,
bumps into Captain Randall. He goes pale
with cursing rage, jumps up, and knocks her down.
In the hush that follows, the minister proclaims
Coloreds aren't welcome here, from this day on.
T.T.'s blue eyes meet hers, sharing her shame.
The colored worshipers, silent and grim,
file out as the organist strikes up a hymn.
  (From "Thus Far by Faith," *The Fields of Praise,* 1996)

"Thus Far by Faith" is a crown of sonnets, a sequence of seven sonnets, each beginning with the last line of the previous one (or a variation upon it), the last sonnet ending with the line that opened the poem. And, like Donne's "Corona," it is a poem about the soul's difficult relationship to faith in tribulation. But it is also the narrative of a small but emblematic event in African American history: the founding of a black church, a Methodist congregation in Kentucky, by former slaves, by one man in particular who became its minister. The seven sonnets, each with a reference to a New Testament verse, begin before the Civil War and Emancipation, and end on Easter Sunday, 1866. Each poem is a self-contained vignette, in which something significant to the narrative is recounted directly, while something else is more obliquely revealed. In the opening sonnet, Uncle Warren's gift for spontaneous preaching (and the local story that moved Nelson toward the poem, about the historical Warren preaching to his mules before he had a congregation) is shown, and his enslaved state is implied; in the fifth, the expulsion of the black parishioners from the white church is straightforward narrative; Captain Randall's fury is followed by the casually dropped detail of the "blue eyes" of the child in Aunt Sally (Warren's wife)'s charge. Sally is looking after a white child, as a nanny, and it's a white child's inadvertent misbehavior which precipitates the expulsion of the black parishioners. Like Tony Harrison, Nelson combines demotic and elevated language, incorporating a discreet use of black dialect into the poem, in the three sestets and one octet where Warren preaches. But these are also the lines which grapple directly with the questions of faith, works, and right action in the face of evil, and those in which the language transcends the narrative, becomes lyrical and figurative: "*Be the stars / what give a twisted generation light*" in the first sonnet. "*Come harvest you'll have love you can give away / and a heart that swells up of its own accord*": the seventh sonnet ends in the opening line of the first one, with the first Easter sermon preached by Warren, in a barn, but not to mules this time: to his own congregation. For Nelson, there seems to be no "argument" between the form and nonstandard English; they are made to seem as relevant to each other as Scripture is to Warren's ability to transcend his status as first a slave and then a powerless freedman (and to protect his wife from insult).

The work of these four poets with the sonnet form constitutes an eloquent proof of its malleability, its diversity: not that the sonnet as a form in itself is "pertinent," but that it lends itself to pertinent topics, to which, by the weight and richness of its history, it adds a counterpoint of what has gone before, setting the contemporary issue into stronger relief.

Younger writers—Julia Alvarez, Jenny Factor, Rafael Campo, Karen Volkman, the Kashmiri-American Aga Shahid Ali, the Ghanian-American Kwame Dawes—have created sonnet sequences exploring English/Spanish bilingualism, homosexual love and visibility, the troubled history of Kashmir, the relationship of poetry to medicine, surreal wordplay stretched and molded by syntax. Any of these topics, like those chosen by Brooks, Rukeyser, Harrison, Nelson, could incite a poetry of "protest" too easily degenerating into polemic. But these poets choosing the sonnet eschew polemic for the perhaps more revolutionary strategy of entering the domain of poetic discourse as protagonists, not antagonists, calling attention to what has frequently been excluded but always is potentially and necessarily present in that space.

Marie Étienne

Marie Étienne, born in Menton in the Alpes-Maritimes, spent her childhood in Indochina, in what is now Vietnam, during World War II and the beginning of the Viet Minh struggle for independence: her father was a French military officer who survived capture by the Japanese. These origins (as well as her father's prison journals) are the basis of her 2002 novel *Sensö: La guerre*, a kaleidoscopic impression of the war and the multiple displacements of a child between cultures, and of her 2007 memoir/fiction *L'Enfant et le soldat.* Her own education continued in France and in Dakar, and she has remained a traveler and an ambassador between literary cultures all her life.

> I could tell you how for a long time I thought my memory was paralyzed: twenty years passed outside France and what have I left of it?
>
> —Take a good look, said my father, take a good look, we're passing the Suez Canal!
>
> I was seven years old, we were standing on the bridge of the boat that was returning from Cochin-China, the water below was far away, I felt lost, perched like a bird, minuscule.
>
> I have forgotten Suez, the significant canal, I've only kept the command, which was not to forget, the sensation of my height above the sea, the uneasiness. How not to fall?
>
> ("Ocean/Emotion," *King of a Hundred Horsemen*)

Many prominent French poets, young, less young, "experimental" and "established," have in common, in the shadow of Mallarmé, not merely the aim of extreme concision but a conscious thrust to banish narrativity from their work. But there are other currents and countermeasures. There is a certain lyricism unabashedly claiming Verlaine's heritage; there is the virtuoso use of invented or inherited constraints by the OuLiPo poets, constraints which paradoxically induce narrative or its semblance; there are the variously broad strokes and wide linguistic horizons of vastly different Francophone poets of African, Arabic, French Canadian, or West Indian heritage whose work is more and more appreciated in France; there are poets incorporating argot, quotidian speech, and street speech with gusto into their work. Marie Étienne, omnivorous reader though she is, cannot easily be placed in any "movement": her work seems sui generis, and this perhaps has to do with the hybridity of her literary origins, both her expatriate childhood and what followed.

From 1979 to 1988, Marie Étienne worked as assistant to the innovative French theater director Antoine Vitez at the Théâtre d'Ivry and the Théâtre National de Chaillot, whose courses on the theater she had followed as part of her doctoral thesis research. Commuting to Paris from a different life in Orléans with a husband and young daughter, her responsibilities included the organization of Monday evening poetry readings that took place on the sets of the theater pieces performed on the other evenings of the week. Étienne was then a well-published "emerging" writer and a frequent contributor to the lively, long-lived, and politically engaged quarterly *Action Poétique*, well placed to integrate poetry-off-the-page into the life of the theater. It was a heady period in French literary life, as it was in the poet's own development, during which *Action Poétique* enjoyed the collaboration of such varied figures as the poet/novelist/mathematician Jacques Roubaud, and the Lacanian historian-journalist Elizabeth Roudinesco. The contributions of aesthetic and political radicals in the arts seemed to be welcome. Vitez, as befits a director of Racine and Molière (and as another artist seeking further integration of disciplines), saw poetry and theater on a continuum. But Étienne was also a chronicler of the daily life of the theater troupe: interactions among actors, stage managers, and the director; the challenges posed by the troupe's physical settings; the pauses and separations (holidays, departures to perform in repertory) which brought the participants back together with renewed energy, increased impatience, or both. More than Vitez's amanuensis, she was one of his privileged interlocutors, his Boswell and dramaturge. She recorded in a series of note-books different aspects of their multiform collaboration: Vitez's written and spoken reflections, her own reactions to the plays and their mise-en-scène, the momentous shift from a bare-bones community theater in Ivry to the monumental Théâtre de Chaillot at the Trocadéro. Vitez's work combined a commitment to the classics with a passionate engagement in socially progressive causes during the years of the student uprisings in France and the Algerian war of independence that put an end to the French colonial presence. Vitez reinterpreted the classics, Greek tragedy in particular, but also the French classics, in the light of current events, and his vision extended to his instruction and direction of young actors at the Conservatoire d'Art Dramatique and the École de Chaillot.

Marie Étienne's collaboration with Vitez followed a five-year period in her life when theater and poetry were the joint subjects of her concentration. Her theatrical engagement was coeval with her attaining greater notice, indeed, with her growing confident self-definition as a writer, which the director—known in a different discipline but actively interested in contemporary poetry—was one of many established figures to encourage. Like plants burgeoning in another part of a garden, her own early books were beginning to appear at this time. Étienne's engagement with poetry (and narrative prose), in part because of the interactive and theatrical context of its development, encompassed from the start the possibility of a polyvocal text, of language as a cue in a choreography of real or imagined motion, of writing that engages in dialogue with other texts, other cultures, other disciplines, incorporating "spoken" dialogue itself into poetry in a way many contemporary French poets have eschewed. The synthesis of the contemporary and the classical, of the tragic and the mundane, of the quotidian transformed by the prisms of myth and history, is present in Marie Étienne's poetry. So is a theatrical framework of invented fixed forms for snatches of narrative that veer from the seemingly ordinary to the surreal, from the urban present to an oneiric time-beyond-time. Several of the sequences in the present book draw on the theater, play with its rituals, utilize dialogue in place of or superseding narration, put the stage itself on stage:

The audience applauds, the professor takes a bow, the audience applauds, the professor takes a bow, the audience applauds, the professor, already standing, who thought the match was over, bends forward once again.

A nasal damsel pipes up to swipe his pittance.

Someone snickers. The damsel is dubious.

No, it's she who doubts:

—To what dawn shall I dedicate my arm, my back, my perfect body?

Objections.

The damsel simpers, an ice cream cone in her hand, Lolita sunglasses astride her nose, while Humpty Dumpty watches her from a few paces away, having made up his mind to.

Music!

The morning fanfare resounds.

Hurry!

Get up, suit up, take one's perch and one's prerogatives.

The news is heard.

—Three days to avoid war!

—Why three days? says astonished Lam, awakening.

("The End and the Beginning,"
King of a Hundred Horsemen)

The ludic and the surreal have always played an important part in Étienne's work, from her debut as a writer. She has kept a lively if distanced or bemused interest in the OuLiPo movement, in which her *Action Poétique* colleague Jacques Roubaud remains a signal figure. She herself is interested more in a philosophical reflection on the direction taken by written texts as they develop than in a "submission," however playful or arbitrary, to form or formula. For her the writer is the "coachman driving the team of horses pulling the carriage," exercising a control kept by awareness of a constant and fruitful tension between the conscious and the unconscious, as well as between content and form.

Marie Étienne now lives in Paris, where she is a frequent contributor to literary and book review journals, in particular the literary critical journal *La Quinzaine littéraire*, for which she has written regularly since 1985, reviewing fiction, literary nonfiction, and poetry. For several years, she wrote a monthly page for the journal *Aujourd'hui Poème*, which she often used to present contemporary foreign poetry in translation to its readership. She has been especially instrumental in bringing the work of Vietnamese and Japanese poets to a French audience.

Étienne is at present the author of eleven books of poems, and of nine books of prose which could be variously classed as fiction, memoir, and cultural history, some partaking of all three. She has edited and introduced two anthologies of contemporary poetry. Her work with Vitez, including transcriptions of her notebooks of the era, resulted in *Antoine Vitez: le roman du théâtre*, a book in a genre Americans would call literary memoir, published in 2000, a decade after the director's death and almost twenty years after their collaboration. It offers an invaluable aperçu of a collaborative artistic endeavor and a signal era in contemporary French theater. Other recent books include the novel *L'Inconnue de la Loire* (2004), *Les Passants intérieurs,* an experimental prose work (2004), *Les Soupirants* (2005), short narratives which upend and parody the expectations of literary pornography, *Dormans,* a book of poetry (2006), and *L'Enfant et le soldat,* an autobiographical novel published in 2006 as well.

The "condition of women" and a subversion of received thought on that subject, is a subtext in more than one of Marie Étienne's books, though rarely is it presented in the context of autobiographical material. Rather, it is implied in the account of a soldier's wife's life in Indochina in the 1940s, or of the narrow horizons facing a young girl in the pre-war French provinces in the novels drawing on her family history. The troublesome connection of a credible woman's persona with the erotics of a Bataille, a Breton, or a Jouve is indicated in the surreal fiction of *Les Soupirants.* An early sequence drawing directly on the poet's theatrical experience is a series of prose-poem letters in the spirit of Ovid's *Héroïdes,* written in the persona of Racine's Bérénice exiled in Iduméa to the imperial Roman lover who banished her. The lyric "I" in Marie Étienne's poetry is a protean, not to say unreliable, narrator, an inveterate storyteller, a speaker constantly subverting the very expectations of the poem in its contemporary guises, yet it (or "she") reasserts just as persistently the possibility of such an "I" having a voice marked as a woman's while engaged in quests and exploration rather than self-examination: the explorer's travel narrative is one of the many "forms" borrowed and transfigured by the poet.

Although the consideration of women's poetry / women's writing as such is somewhat alien to many French women writers (at least those not associated with the "Psychanalyse et politique" movement, who themselves disavow the term "feminist"), Étienne did a considerable study of twentieth-century French women poets for a chapter on the subject in the 2003 anthology *Beyond French Feminisms*. One of her discoveries perusing anthologies was exactly that of the American feminist writer Joanna Russ in her own assessment of canonical English anthologies published before 1980: there was a uniform, modest percentage of women poets included, but, while the presence of individual male poets was constant from one anthology to the next, women included would disappear and be replaced in the persistent 5 to 10 percent. Women poets' place in contemporary French poetry is still an uneasy one, as compared with Anglophone poetry, and also with Francophone Canadian poetry, where their highly significant role in the creation of a specifically Canadian modernism is universally acknowledged. Only fourteen women, Canadians and other non-French Francophones included, figure in the 2000 edition of the 670-page Gallimard pocket anthology of French poetry of the second half of the twentieth century, containing work by 150 poets born between 1907 and 1950 (with only two women born in the last decade of this time span). This can be contrasted with a considerable presence of women fiction writers and literary essayists, in every register from the detective novel to all flavors of avant-garde. Given the exaggerated care with which the editorial borders seem to be guarded, it is paradoxical that in France, poetry itself has suffered even greater critical segregation and exclusion—in the literary press, on bookshop and library shelves—than it has in the United States, nor is it alternatively propagated and disseminated by well-attended public readings. This might well constitute an additional reason for a writer, a woman writer in particular, to prefer not to confine or define herself by a single literary genre.

Marie Étienne has always composed poetry and prose alternately or simultaneously, seeing the genre barrier as arbitrary in many instances. In an extended essay in a recent issue of the journal *Formes poétiques contemporaines,* she examined the prose poem as genre, with its attractions and pitfalls, and scrutinized its uses by a variety of contemporaries. She resists the idea of a "collection" of poems, seeing in each book of her poetry as much of a unity as in a work of fiction, and concomitantly regards some of her fiction as approaching the long poem in prose. Indeed, "fiction" is as limiting a definition of her work in prose as "collection" might be of her carefully constructed poetic works. Some of these books could more properly be called extended memoir than novels: extended, that is, into an individual or familial past, but with an elaboration that has more to do with acknowledged imagination and linguistic invention than documentary reconstruction. This is a genre that readers of contemporary French writing will associate with (for example) Marguerite Duras, who shared, albeit in a different generation, Marie Étienne's experience of a Southeast Asian childhood, and with Marguerite Yourcenar's nonfiction re-creations of her maternal and paternal family histories, which partake necessarily of the fictional; but also with the contemporary work of writers as divergent as Patrick Modiano, Richard Millet, Hervé Guibert, Leila Sebbar, and Hélène Cixous. Other books of Étienne's make use of formal experimentation in a stylized and elegant manner that has little to do with the depiction of a presumed reality. Both the Prix Mallarmé-winning *Anatolie* and the recent *Dormans,* unified books labeled "poetry," alternate verse, including rhymed short-lined quatrains and decasyllabic dixains (a form associated with the metaphysical-erotic "blasons" of Maurice Scève) with pages of prose narrative and prose poems.

> Daybreak it's time for bathing and grooming
> Which all takes place outdoors on a wooden
> Dock, closed off at the end by a curtain
> Which the rare strollers, if they're curious
> If they have a taste for tropical scenes
> Lift up as they pass by without dawdling
> They're frequent clients they're from neighboring

Villages, you might be on the banks of
The Ganges
        No modesty, what counts is
The ritual of purification
    (From "The Bath," a section of a longer sequence,
            "The Ebony Mare")

Exploration in the most classic and adventurous sense, contemporary urban life, the myths, tales, and customs of real and invented peoples, alternate as in a fugue in both books.

Roi des cent cavaliers (published in France in 2002) exists in the territory Étienne has created between poetry and prose, with all of the poem's compression and making full use of its fertile paradoxes. It is a unified book consisting of nine sequences that enigmatically consider war, human relations, sex, nature, the contemporary world, and its intersecting cultures, and the poet's own (international) history. Structurally, the book pivots on two numbers: fourteen, since each individual poem is a "prose (or prose-poem) sonnet," each of whose lines is a discrete sentence, and ten, along with its multiple, one hundred, as each sequence or "chapter" is composed of ten such sonnets, and the book as a whole, with its (numbered) titles and annotations included, comprises a hundred sections. The text is porous: there are collagings or interpellations of Marina Tsvetaeva, T. S. Eliot, Tristan Tzara, and others: Tsvetaeva's voice, or Étienne's re-creation of it, alternates with the narrator's in one sequence. Two of the most seemingly "surreal" sequences, each of which begins with the evocation of a painter and his surroundings, are, in fact, also descriptive "fugues" on themes in the work of two contemporary French graphic artists, Gaston Planet and François Dilasser.

He paints on brown wrapping paper, Canson paper, newspaper. Paper that's been oiled, gouached, scratched.

He paints on glass, panel, pieces of cardboard. Free, hybrid, light canvas, mattress ticking.

With oil paints. Vinyl, wash drawing, dye. Pencil, pastel, India ink. Printers' ink or ink for pens. And watercolors.

By rubbing, creasing, scratching, with cutter, pebble, with fingernail, matchstick.

He paints landscapes at different times of day.

He needs solitude.

Only in this case do apple trees, children, rocks, low stone walls, become deformed delirious, not in the grip of the fantastic, but the real, to which he submits.

The stretchers have marked the canvas with a cross.

The canvas has a flaw.

A drop ran down, and suddenly, an army of drops need to run, they must be hurled.

He paints or he writes quickly, inhabited by urgency, he takes the picture or the text by surprise, he battles with them, the image springs up from below.

("A Witness Disappears,"
King of a Hundred Horsemen)

Who are the two protagonists, female and male, with vaguely Southeast Asian names, venturing through the jungles of fable, the architecture of dreams—or the airport in Atlanta, Georgia? Alternating with them is a first-person narrator whose "war diary" resembles most closely quotidian life in contemporary Paris, but whose experiences veer sharply away from the "possible" just when a reader begins to take her for the writer's avatar. Linking them all is "the child," an interlocutor, who passes in and out of all their stories. The book as a whole reflects, as in a mosaic of shattered mirrors, many of the writer's ongoing preoccupations: the potentially theatrical nature of writing on the page; the simultaneous construction/deconstruction of narrative; gender; the juxtaposition of Orient and Occident; an eroticism that is at once physical and cerebral; the extension of the limits of genre (poetry / prose / dramatic writing); an interpenetration of the quotidian and the foreign, in which the most "exotic" journeys become ordinary, and the most ordinary displacements partake of the disquieting and the strange.

Faith and Works

Marilyn Nelson's The Fields of Praise

Marilyn Nelson is one of a generation of African American poets who came of age in the 1960s and early 1970s, upon whom the pressure to write from a communal and specifically virile rage was felt as strongly as the cold draft from the shutting doors of established literary journals. Black community was reinterpreted as black separatism: no less a poet than Gwendolyn Brooks, whose entire oeuvre chronicled the life of Chicago's South Side from World War II on, with a particular but in no way exclusive emphasis on portraits of less-than-remarkable women, the elderly, the un-picturesque, felt obliged to publish an auto-critical credo taking herself to task for not having envisioned a specifically black readership for that work. At least temporarily, she abandoned the formal, linguistic, and psychological complexity of her work of the forties, fifties, and early sixties for something more accessible and clearly laudatory of revolutionary black youth. This may only have (also temporarily) perplexed the younger black poets (like Marilyn Nelson) for whom the complexity of Brooks's narratives, the richness of her language, illustrated precisely a way that African American voices, and their way with words inflected, as black English is, with Elizabethan playfulness and Miltonic measure, entered into the discourse of American verse.

The Fields of Praise is a mid-career selection from four earlier books, combined with new work. Rather than arrange the poems chronologically, Nelson has chosen to order them thematically: roughly, the maternal and paternal principles; a multigenerational African American family history; spiritual parables; meditations on the nature of good and evil. Still, the book traces a thematic and formal development, as the poet's worldview opens out through her chosen subjects. The concentration of the first forty pages is on the poet's childhood intermingled with her own first child's infancy, on the quotidian constrictions of a young mother's life, and, framing those, on the configuration of a kind of Magna Mater growing from images of the poet's mother and of the speaker herself to a usually beneficent but potentially destructive locus of creative energy, in ironic contrast with the real young mother's daily rounds. These poems are largely from the poet's first two collections: in the context of Nelson's later work (and in that of African American poetry of the seventies and early eighties), a reader is surprised by the absence of the "macrohistorical" world's events. But the energy and wit of these poems, even their occasional frank (comic) claustrophobia, has its source in feminist writing of those same decades, often perceived as largely white, but including the earlier work of Audre Lorde, Lucille Clifton, and Toi Derricotte, as well as Nelson, for all of whom the perception of childbirth and child-rearing *as* events with histories, both oppressive and epiphanic (and most often traced back through women's own mothers' stories) was the center of a worldview:

> I want to run, but the baby's an anvil,
> my breasts are concrete blocks,
> I stagger under the weight
> In the getaway car the baby claws
> at my hands; I fight to keep the wheels
> on a track that bends back on itself . . .
> . . . .
> The blank picture windows
> make this a room of trick mirrors:
> as I rush to pick him up
> I see a pigtailed little girl
> arms held wide for balance
> in Mama's size 10 high-heeled shoes.
>   ("The Dangerous Carnival")

There is a shock of change upon encountering the "paternal" side of this diptych, which is not only collective rather than individual, but a literal evocation of "sky-fathers"—African American pilots of the all-black 477th Bombardiers and the 332nd Fighter Group: the "Tuskegee Airmen," of whom the poet's father was one. Written later than most of the "motherhood" poems, this sequence plots the intersection of three kinds of history: that of the American Air Force in World War II, that of African American experience and worldview changed (or underscored) by military service, and the individual stories of black men who flew in combat. The impact on black men of military service in World War II, the segregation experienced within the armed forces, the tragic irony of racism in the lives of returning servicemen, were central themes in Gwendolyn Brooks's first two books five decades earlier. Nelson's airmen, though, are individuated in a different (and indeed more familial) way, in narratives and dramatic monologues (wrought from informal interviews) counterpointing the daily routines, triumphs and losses of men at war with the incontrovertible weight of race in their lives, from the "full-bird colonel" mistaken for a porter in an airport to the squadron of black officers imprisoned for refusing to sign an agreement not to enter the officers' club—while German POWs smoked and laughed outdoors.

The Tuskegee Airmen sequence was originally included in *The Homeplace*, Nelson's 1990 collection in which it followed a narrative sequence tracing the poet's maternal line through four generations, beginning with Diverne, a slave great-great-grandmother brought from Jamaica (and the white landowner's scion who fathered her son). This juxtaposition, with its complex perspective on African American history, also highlighted the poet's stylistic range, moving from the sonnets and other fixed forms used for the multigenerational narrative to the deceptively limpid short-lined free verse of the airmen's stories. Not unlike the British poet Tony Harrison in his use of West Yorkshire speech in *The School of Eloquence*, or Derek Walcott choosing a speaker of Caribbean patois to narrate "The Schooner Flight," Nelson demonstrates how American Black English is served eloquently by the forms:

> *She think she something, stuck-up island bitch.*
> Chopping wood, hanging laundry on the line,
> and tantalizingly within his reach

she honed his body's yearning to a keen
sharp point. And on that point she balanced life.
That hoe Diverne think she Marse Tyler's wife.
                    ("Balance")

An entire section in the new book contains the "Homeplace"
poems, completed by a newer virtuoso crown of sonnets drawn
from the history of a black Methodist chapel in Kentucky,
founded by a former slave, who first tried out his preaching
skills while driving mules:

> *Beloved, stop your grumbling. Be the stars*
> *what give a twisted generation light.*
> *That's what the book say. But old Satan roars*
> *louder, sometimes, than Master. He say, Hate*
> *the whip-hand and the yoke. Why be a fool?*
> *The Lord Hisself were tempted, Brother Mule.*
>   ("Thus Far By Faith")

Underlying the personal/political and the historical/narra-
tive, there is, from Nelson's earliest work on, a theme of spiritual quest structuring the poems: a search for the divine in the
quotidian balanced by a meditation on the nature of evil in a
spectrum going from childish betrayals and individual bad faith
to the authorship and agency of the Middle Passage and the
Final Solution. Deist or pagan in the book's beginning, merging
with the ecstatic and pragmatic Christianity of the freed slaves
and their descendants in "The Homeplace," this quest takes an
enigmatic turn in the section entitled "Hermitage." Nelson here
frames a series of psalms and lucid parables about a contemporary Desert Father within the story of a woman's rediscovery of
a man she'd loved in student days, now become a contemplative
priest-hermit. In a canticle of twelve five-line stanzas, she braids
the obligatory metamorphosis of the woman's passion with the
monk's yearning toward God in the erotically charged vocabulary of the Song of Songs:

> How beautiful You are, my Love,
> how beautiful You are.
>   Your changeful eyes,

the humble grace with which you move
your hands, your laughter, your surprise.
Your listening silences. Your God, who dies.
("A Canticle for Abba Jacob")

Nelson has written eloquently (notably in an essay published
in the *Gettysburg Review* in 1995) of her own relationship, as an
African American poet, with the canonical tradition and with the
counter-tradition of the sixties' Black Arts movement. These
writers had denied the validity of a black radicalism—that of the
Harlem Renaissance, of Robert Hayden, James Baldwin, and
Gwendolyn Brooks—which positioned itself as a necessary *part*
and *development* of the canon, and thus challenged that canon's
power to exclude their varied voices. Nelson was moved, in both
senses, by the impulse which led a poet like Amiri Baraka to
attempt, instead of that dialectic of inclusion, the creation of a
separatist Black Aesthetic. And yet, as she asks herself in her
essay, "How can a poet survive such a radical self-amputation?" In
an early poem, "Women's Locker Room," the interruption by a
beautiful white intruder of her solitude in the shower leads the
speaker to fantasize:

> I could freeze her name in an ice cube,
> bottle the dirt from her footsteps
> with potent graveyard dust
> . . . .
> I jump, grimace, divide like an amoeba
> into twin rages that stomp around
> with their lips stuck out
> then come suddenly face to face.
> They see each other and know that they
> are mean mamas.
>
> Then I bust out laughing
> and let the woman live.

Her own choice seems here to have already been made:
humor, yes, but also the self-reflectiveness of a double voice and
double vision which establishes a decolonizing dialectic with the
canon: a choice also made by poets like Yusef Komunyakaa, Rita
Dove, Michael Harper, and Thylias Moss. But "double vision" is

a strength of Nelson's work in more than a cultural context: it grounds her understanding of the mutual sources of erotic and spiritual longing, of the ways the universe reveals its workings in quotidian perceptions. It is enacted in her explorations of the parallel possibilities of free and fixed forms, in the way she creates lyric which rises in eloquent cadenza from a narrative, and heightened language which is rooted in demotic speech:

> Shut up, close your eyes,
> and wake into a new way of seeing.
> Go into yourself, look around.
>
> And if what you see there isn't beautiful
> don't stop smoothing, polishing, cutting away until
> you are *wholly yourself, nothing but pure light.*
> ("The Plotinus Suite," *X Enneads*)

Tectonic Shifts

Alicia Ostriker's The Crack in Everything

Alicia Ostriker's work joins the humanitarian's unalienated élan to ameliorate suffering and share what's of value, which energizes progressive political engagement, to the humanist's hunger to re-engage with and continually re-define intellectual (specifically literary, also spiritual) traditions: the pedagogical passion. She is a Blake scholar and a Bible scholar, a feminist critic whose work continues to germinate a wider-branching, inclusive literary purview, a Jew whose writings are informed by while they interrogate that heritage and history. She is a mother and a teacher. She is also an important American poet, whose writing is enriched, enriches its readers, by all those sometimes conflicting identities.

The Crack in Everything is her eighth collection of poems (and her eleventh book). Ostriker is not a "difficult" poet, demanding of the reader a primary concern with the construction (or deconstruction) of literary edifices: she is a Socratic poet who engages the reader in complex examinations by means of simple questions, deceptively simple declarative sentences.

> I picked the books to come along with me
> On this retreat at the last moment
> ("After Illness")

> In Chicago, Petersburg, Tokyo, the dancers
> Hit the floor running
> ("Saturday Night")

> We say things in this class. Like why it hurts.
> ("The Class")

I called him fool, she said.
It just slipped out
("Alice Before Her Widowhood")

A series of homages to other ordinary/extraordinary
women makes a kind of framework to the book's first half. Two
dramatic monologues, spoken by a middle-class and a working-
class woman, confronting the end (or not) of marriage, are followed, mirrored, by two magnificent portraits of known artists:
the painter Alice Neel and the poet May Swenson, in which
Ostriker meticulously details the way various "ordinarinesses"
can coalesce into genius.

After a vivid introductory stanza in which all the senses are
called to witness, in counterpoint with a litany of American
brand names, Neel, quintessential urban American painter,
speaks (through the poet) for herself:

You got to understand, this existence is it,
I blame nobody, I just paint, paint is thicker than water,
Blood, or dollars. My friends and neighbors are made
Of paint, would you believe it, paintslabs and brushstrokes
Right down to the kishkes, as my grandfather would say.
Like bandaged Andy, not smart enough to duck

Palette knife jabs, carnation, ochre, viridian.
("The Studio")

and continues, relentlessly, to recount her descent into and
emergence from mental illness before the poem ends.

Swenson's portrait, like her own poems, is structured on
word-/eye-perfect observation: of a tortoise, which "generates"
the image of the child-poet examining the animal, and the mature poet's own not-un-tortoise-like, equally cannily observed
physical presence. "Amphibian, crustacean?" Ostriker asks, to
begin, and concludes, two pages later, "It's friendly. Really a
mammal." A modest inference to which Swenson would readily
have assented, as she'd have been pleased to be glimpsed in her
own naturalist's glass.

These ordinary/extraordinary strains meet in the book's
long centerpiece, "The Book of Life," addressed to sculptor

Sheila Solomon, whose work readers won't know as they do Neel's and Swenson's. The theme of the poet's and sculptor's correspondences/differences, as artists, as friends, as Jews, as parents, interweave with descriptions of the sculptor's work and workplace, and with the story of a third friend, who died of cancer in early middle age:

> You started the eight-foot goddess
> The year Cynthia spent dying
> The same year you were sculpting
> Her small bald head
> Fretting you couldn't get
> The form . . .
>> ("The Book of Life")

In five sections, seven dense pages, "The Book of Life" was more, to me, like the notebook (writers' "books of life") from which a complex poem might be drawn. "Figurative sculpture is dead," the sculptor is told, but persists in her own (figurative, majestic) vision. This poem, with its doubled or tripled levels of narration and description, left me wishing for what I equate with the figurative in poetry: the fixed structure of accentual-syllabic form to "order" its plunges and ascents through the sculptor's studio and garden, the friends' shared history.

(Ostriker is, in general, a poet whose formal strategies inspire confidence, and seem the outer manifestation of the poem's intentions, whether in the Sapphic echoes of the epithalamion "Extraterrestrials" triplet stanzas, the clear-cut free-verse couplets of the May Swenson tribute, the Augustan rhymed pentameter, witty and elegiac, of "After the Reunion.")

Ostriker is a teacher—by vocation, one feels, not just economic necessity: a poet/scholar who teaches not only "creative writing," but the creative *reading* that sustains the republic of letters. Many poets and novelists teach: Ostriker (along with Toi Derricotte and Marie Ponsot) is one of the few who has written about, recognized, and re-created the pedagogic relationship as one of the quintessentially human connections, as fit a subject for poetry as erotic love or the changes spring rings on a meadow. Her students, as individuals or cohered into a class, are present in a group of these poems, where the dynamic that fuels a class's work together is examined—not a lecturer imprinting young minds blank as new tapes, but a multivocal conversation, a collective expedition:

> All semester they brought it back
> A piece at a time, like the limbs of Osiris.
> ("The Nature of Beauty")

Generous as she is, Ostriker can permit herself the rueful professorial aside that the one student who "gets" Emily Dickinson, after the teacher's inspired cadenza on her poems, is "the boy / Who'd had four years of Latin / In high school and loved Virgil" ("Frowning at Emily"). And, activist as she has always been, she cannot view the university in a vacuum, peopled only by students and teachers. "Lockout," the poem which opens the "university" sequence, is largely spoken by a middle-aged Latino security guard, aware of how the imported hegemony of English has inflected his life, the lives of the continent's native peoples.

The contemplative poem, "After Illness," strategically placed early in the section following "The Book of Life," and before the teacher/student poems, makes graceful reference to gratuitous, inevitable bodily destiny, different but equally mortal for each individual:

> What is a dance without some mad randomness
> Making it up? Look, getting sick
> Was like being born.
> They singled you out from among the others
> With whom you were innocently twirling,
> Doing a samba across the cumulonimbus,
>
> They said *you*, they said *now*.

Two pages, two sections later, still in a cropped triplet stanza, the poet/speaker refers to "my mastectomy"—but in a subordinate clause of a sentence whose (conditional) object, and objective is "mourning" and "feeling" as potential mental foci of her sought solitude, counterbalanced by imagined indulgence of an improvident infatuation; the conclusion is that any consciously determined subject of meditation "By definition isn't it." In this elegant philosophical play, "mastectomy" seems to enter almost offhandedly into the discourse, until the reader realizes how it informs the earlier stanzas about the dance of randomness, the falling into the body of illness as we've "fallen into" our bodies at birth. The balance between the raw, unresolved mourning for Cynthia in "The Book of Life" and this almost ludic intrusion of the harsh word "mastectomy" with its vulnerable first-person possessive pronoun, prepares the reader for the book's concluding and conclusive achievement, "The Mastectomy Poems," a twelve-poem sequence examining the writer's own experience of breast cancer.

In the book's preceding sections, Ostriker has displayed a virtuoso register of styles, voices, forms: the dramatic monologue / word-portrait; the aphoristic or fable-like narrative in meter and rhyme; the pedagogical "I" addressing a plural "thou"; the quotidian anecdotal which shifts subtly into the meditative or the surreal. She deploys all of these in "The Mastectomy Poems" to create a mosaic of a woman's changing inner and outer life as she undergoes this ordeal (become so horrifyingly common as to resemble a rite of passage). All the while, given the book's structure, in the augmented formal echoes of its preceding themes, she reiterates as subtext that the breast cancer survivor is, chastened and changed, the same woman, the same artist and citizen, that she was before: she who praises other women (here, a breast surgeon) in the exercise of their vocations:

> I shook your hand before I went.
> Your nod was brief, your manner confident,
> A ship's captain, and there I lay, a chart
> Of the bay, no reefs, no shoals.
> ("4. Mastectomy")

a sensual/social woman:

> . . . I told a man *I've resolved*
> *To be as sexy with one breast*
> *As other people are with two*
> And he looked away.
> ("7. Wintering")

a lyric economist of meter and rhyme:

> And now the anesthesiologist
> Tells something reassuring to my ear—
> And a red moon is stripping to her waist—
> How good it is, not to be anywhere.
> ("2. The Gurney")

a teacher and member of the academic community:

> First classes, the sun is out, the darlings
> Troop in, my colleagues
> Tell me I look normal. I am normal.
> ("8. Normal")

Always, though, underneath the surface, under the "Black and red China silk jacket," is the shocked, transformed body, the "skinny stripe," "short piece of cosmic string" of the mastectomy scar, sign of escape and *memento mori* at once.

Omnipresent too, the scar's double, is the lost breast, also with a double significance, first as instrument of pleasure, self-contained sustenance, bodily benignity, badge of responsible womanhood:

> My right guess, my true information

transformed into a kind of time bomb, storehouse of explosives, inert but dangerous matter:

> Jug of star-fluid, breakable cup—
> Someone shoveled your good and bad crumbs
> Together into a plastic container
> For breast tissue is like silicon
> ("5. What Was Lost")

And the breast, or the ghost breast, marks mortality now even more than the scar:

> *Carry me mama.* Sweetheart,
> I hear you. I will come.
> ("11. The River")

the poem concludes: the generative constant rescue mission of maternity thus transformed into the poet's prescience of death.

Abruptly, the sequence's next, last poem begins and ends with the speaker back in the quotidian world of work and talk: "Bookbag on my back, I'm out the door"—a teacher again, with the vivacity and accoutrements of a young student in her self-description. "Winter turns to spring, the way it does," and she unthinkingly answers the anxious "How are you feeling?" with anecdotes about family and work. "The woman under the surface" is back on the surface, in her disguise as an ordinary worker-bee, an "ordinariness" like that which camouflages the genius of Swenson and Neel in their poem-portraits. But this section is entitled "Epilogue"—which gives us the double message that, despite the brisk exit-line, the poem's "real" conclusion is the haunted one of "The River."

One section of "The Mastectomy Poems" has an epigraph—referring to "ordinary women"—from a poem by Lucille Clifton. Not at all parenthetically, Clifton too was treated for breast cancer, a few years after Ostriker. Some, only some, of the other contemporary American women writers who are living with, or who have succumbed to breast cancer are, in no particular order: Pat Parker, Audre Lorde, Susan Sontag, Maxine Kumin, Eve Kosofsky Sedgwick, Judith Moffett, Penelope Austin, Edith Konecky, Hilda Raz, Patricia Goedicke, June Jordan, Grace Paley, myself: black, white, Jewish; fat, thin, and middling; lesbian, straight (and middling); childless and multiparous—to borrow the title of a poem by Melvin Dixon about friends lost to AIDS, "And These Are Just a Few."

The Crack in Everything: is it a shift in the earth's tectonic plates, the purposeful Zen flaw in a ceramic vase which individualizes its perfection, the long pink keloid ridge on a newly flat chest? All of the above. This is not a polemic, a book with an aim, a recovery manual. It reaffirms the poet's unique and contradictory role, at once storyteller and witness, s/he who makes of language not a prison but a prism, refracting and re-combining the spectrum of human possibilities.

Emmanuel Moses

Emmanuel Moses was born in Casablanca in 1959, the son of a French-educated German Jew and a French Jew of Polish descent, one a historian of philosophy and the other a painter. He spent his early childhood in France, lived from the age of ten until his mid-twenties in Israel, where he studied history at the Hebrew University of Jerusalem, and then returned to Paris, where he still lives. He is the author of eight collections of poems, most recently *D'Un perpetuel hiver* (Gallimard, 2009) and *Figure rose* (Flammarion, 2006, which received one of the annual Prix de poésie de l'Académie française), and of eight novels and collections of short fiction. Another poetry collection, *L'Animal*, will appear in 2010. Fluent in four languages, Moses is a translator into French of contemporary Hebrew fiction and poetry, notably of Yehuda Amichai and, recently, Agi Mishol; he edited anthologies of modern poetry in Hebrew for the publishers Obsidiane and Gallimard. He also translates from the German and from the English, including C. K. Williams, Raymond Carver, Gabriel Levin, and younger poets like the 2007 National Poetry Series winner Donna Stonecipher.

A polyglot whose experience of the world comes as much from travel and human intercourse as from books, from an interrogation of the past which coexists with his experience of the present, Emmanuel Moses is a kind of *Poète sans frontières*. While some contemporary French poets eschew geographical specificity, a perennial subject of Moses' poems is the crossing and the porosity of actual borders, geographical and temporal. A (Proustian?) train of thought set in motion by the placement of a park bench, the stripe of sunlight on a brick wall, will move the speaker and the poem itself from Amsterdam to Jerusalem,

from a boyhood memory to a nineteenth-century chronicle,
from Stendhal to the Shoah.

> Hush. The dead are looking at us with their black and white
>   eyes. They prowl
> Like vagabonds, like the moon.
> Light all the lights, uncork the best wine.
> Perhaps, little demon, they'll leave with the fog.
> I rode my bicycle in a cemetery. I picked asters
> And I thought of you. The sky was blue, the earth already
>   autumnal. In an
> Old cemetery, and behind the iron gate, people put their
> Hats back on.
>
> ("The Year of the Dragon" VI)

A subtle irony permeates Moses' work, even (or especially) at
moments meant to be self-reflective or romantic, an irony applied to the events of history as readily as to the events of a single young or aging man's life. It is clear in Moses' poems as in
his fiction that the macro-events of "history" are made up of the
minuscule events of individual existence, and that they must be
perceived as such to be understood. The breadth of the poet's
reading and his intimate relationship with architecture, music,
and painting inform his work and populate it with unexpected
interlocutors: Chopin, Buxtehude, Fragonard, Breughel—or a
London barman, or a Turkish woman pharmacist.

References to diaspora and displacement, to individual histories involving plural geographies and languages, are ubiquitous in this body of work. Moses creates a fluidity of time as well
as place as these texts move across the Europe of his imagination: Napoleon's invasion of Slovenia, the Palazzo Farnese
(which currently houses the French Embassy in Rome), the
death of Chopin, even the Crucifixion, come into focus. The
quintessentially cosmopolitan Istanbul is the setting for what
seems to be an amorous idyll; Majorca becomes the impetus for
a retrospective reflection on cultures crossing in transit. "Letters
from Brandenburg"—the state surrounding Berlin, identified
with Bach—illustrates Moses' geographical and temporal jump-
cutting, as its six sections (mirroring the concertos?) move from
childhood recollection to reflections on human communica-

tion to the abrupt, oblique description of a pogrom. As well as recalling Bach, Brandenburg was the site of the imprisonment by the Germans of the French Résistant poet André Frénaud, who published a series of "Poèmes de Brandebourg" written during his incarceration between 1940 and 1942. The work of Frénaud, who died in 1993, is a touchstone for Moses, and most French readers would see Frénaud as one recipient of these "Letters." Berlin's history haunts the lovers' bed in "Royal Blue" as well. The "Riverbend Passage" sequence is at once more lyric and linguistically ludic, though in a minor key and somber tone.

> Don't let the man in black
> take me away with him
>
> cowbells/opera
> . . . .
> There was once a time when sorrow lay down on me
> as if it wished to warm me
> truly it troubled my spirit
> I was
> Biblical
> . . . .
> The child fears water and bees
> he watches helicopters winch up cows
> his life is you
> bicephalous
> in the mountain pastures again
> . . . .
> From Badland to Deadwood
> the man is on my heels
> don't let him take me away on his black charger
> or aboard the black convoy
> the interlife express

Reading it, and, even more, translating it, I could perceive it as an homage to or dialogue with another Jewish poet without borders, Paul Celan.

The fluid and ironic "Mr. Nobody" persona first appeared briefly in a 2003 collection, to which he gave the title *Dernières nouvelles de Monsieur Néant*. He reappears at much greater length in a sequence of these more recent poems. "Néant" can be translated as "Nothingness," as in the Englishing of Sartre's doorstopper. But "Nothingness" is a doorstopper of a word all by itself in English: after reading a half-dozen or more poems about him, Emmanuel Moses' persona emerges as much more of an "everyman / no man" (a Northern European everyman) than an avatar of the existential void.

> Walking along the row of yew-trees
> Mr. Nobody thinks of his old patronym
>
> a name destined for chronic sorrow
> and drink
>
> he sees those hotel rooms again
> the damp-stained wallpaper
>
> the smudged panes
> which diffused a permanent false daylight
>
> Copenhagen, Göteberg, Bremen
> ("Mr. Nobody's Travels")

He seems to me to be present even in poems that don't bear his name, "small i," for example, and, in a register finally eschewing self-mockery, "Towards Buxtehude." He is a Chaplinesque (even Woody Allen-esque, and, why not, a touch of Joseph Roth in the Hôtel Tournon?) reassessment of the diasporic, elegiac, and history-haunted speaker of many of the other poems: disappointed in love, allergic to most of humanity, but endlessly rewriting a play for myriad characters in a series of temporary residences.

Moses cultivates a formal fluidity in his poems. Some, in French as in translation, are fairly straightforward open-form lyrics or narratives, which may on occasion ("On Ugliness" is an example) open a "frame story" only to veer away and out of the frame.

> Beauty underlying ugliness
> is a hackneyed subject
> further into the thought
> one finds ugliness again
> but fundamental
> a hard and arid soil with nothing more to hide

this is what a redheaded girl with blue eyes writes down
on a blank page of her travel journal
she just passed a quiet night at the hotel Krasnapolsky
—fate's hotel—
she is having breakfast in the mythical winter garden
feeling chic and a bit outdated

Other poems incorporate prose passages, or are made up of pared, short, near-syllabic stanzas. Some are deliberately, enigmatically fragmentary. On the subject of this choice, he has written:

For me, the fragment is something that has been torn off. This violence is at the heart of the writing process, or so I feel. It is a displacement and also a dislocation. What is being created thus? A kind of golem, brimming with destructive powers. You still feel the phantom entity from which the scrap has been detached. The result is a text containing pain and a foolish hope for a healing. I wanted to speak about the mystery contained in the fragment and the imagination it stimulates in the reader's mind but that aspect seems now to me superficial, anecdotal. The fragment is both the result of a mutilation (of the uninterrupted flow of language) and the hope for a miracle: the restoration of its lost unity. (Interview conducted by Donna Stonecipher for chicagopostmodernpoetry.com, 2006)

Many of the poems in his 2009 collection relate, directly or indirectly, to the life and death of Stéphane Moses, the poet's father. Stéphane Moses was born in Berlin in 1931, but educated (in French) in Morocco from the age of six onwards, to pursue his university studies in France. A secular youth, from a confluence of European Jewish cultures decimated by the Shoah, he began his inquiries into Jewish tradition and philosophy when a student at the École Normale Supérieure in the 1950s, as part of the "Jewish philosophical renewal" exemplified by the work of Léon Askénazi, André Neher, and Emmanuel Levinas. He became in his turn an historian and analyst of nineteenth- and early twentieth-century European Jewish thought: his writings on Walter Benjamin, Kafka, Celan, Levinas, Gershom Scholem, and

Franz Rosenzweig are preeminent in the field in France. He died in 2007, after years of cancer treatment. The writer son's regard and love for his scholar father permeate much of his work, but the poems written in 2006–2008 in particular address him, reflect on his history, and compose his elegy, from the thoughtful and ultimately celebratory "The Terrace" and "Alive" to the oblique and deranging "Funeral Supper," a sequence that seems to exemplify a description Moses gave of his own work:

> the obscurity of the impulse seems to occupy an important place in the genesis, something that is veiled, that evades any precise form, a fugitive of a sort and ending in light: something has appeared, at the end of the process, has been shaped by daylight, has come to existence, to a dense and light existence . . . (Interview, chicagopostmodernpoetry.com, 2006)

Moses' choice of George Herbert for an epigraph is one entrance for a reader into the disquiet of this poem: not only an acknowledgment that the most naked confrontation of the poetic imagination with the fact of death may have been that of the English poets now called Metaphysical, but an attempt to draw from and revivify the energy of that face-off.

English poets of the seventeenth century, Frénaud, the French Résistant mystic, Celan and his reconstitution of the contemporary lyric in a language that would always be as much inimical as native, Yehuda Amichai after years of a translator's intimacy—as well as Walter Benjamin, Victor Hugo, and a cinematic overlay of one landscape, one era, on another: these are some of the landmark reference points for Moses and thence for his readers. Yet, despite his multilingual erudition, the dizzying range of his interlocutors, and his obvious pleasure (not in the least doctrinal) in formal experimentation, Moses is a poet with a direct and almost intimate address to the reader who engages with his work: in turn wry, melancholy, funny, self-deprecating, mercurial, fraternal.

Knowledge as a Source of Joy

Marie Ponsot

In her poetry, Marie Ponsot negotiates an edgy territory of loss and discovers it to share a border with the breathtaking landscape of intellectual freedom. The skill in her deployment of prosody is such that one need not remark upon it. A careful reader notices that her words mean what they have always said: every inflection and connotation rippling through the common usage from a point of origin has been accounted for. She teaches us thought's verbal anatomies the way a mother (she would permit the simile) teaches what she knows, not from a syllabus, but in the context of conversation, storytelling, even admonition: loving discourse. Ponsot's poetry is always demanding, but it is never "difficult" in the contemporary critical sense. Rigorous and generous with readers, it is unsparing in what it indicates as it shares what it loves.

One of the delicious paradoxes of Marie Ponsot's work is its examination of the double consciousness of a writer who is bilingual (English and French, with a strong background in Latin) in culture as well as in usage, but in whose writing that profoundly international culture is annealed to a very specific sense of place. Though Paris and other French and North African as well as varied North American landscapes are significant in her work, Ponsot is primarily one of the most eloquent poets of New York City, one whom I'd not hesitate to place alongside Hart Crane, Muriel Rukeyser, and Frank O'Hara in her realization of an urban poetics, in the way in which her work inhabits and is inhabited by this city in particular. For Ponsot, New York is not only Manhattan but that "other" New York of "the outer boroughs," in her case Queens, where she grew up, and where she spent decades teaching at Queens College and raising, mostly single-handedly, her seven children.

The poet was born Marie Birmingham in New York on April 21, 1921: her parents, William and Marie (Candee) Birmingham, were a wine and spirits importer and a schoolteacher, of families long established in the city. She has one brother. At first educated in the New York public school system, she received her B.A. from St. Joseph's College for Women, Brooklyn, in 1940 (at nineteen) and an M.A. from Columbia University in seventeenth-century English literature in 1941. She lived and worked on her own in Manhattan during the war years, from bookselling at Brentano's to being a production manager of juvenile books at Thomas Crowell & Co., writing and reading in the ferment of new voices, the emergence of the first literally post-modernist generation. Possibly the figures in the "classic" modernist movement to have the greatest presence in her development were H.D. and Djuna Barnes, both marginalized by their gender, life choices, and the emerging epic ambitions of their work, both of whose books the young poet purchased as they appeared, read, reflected upon (and both of whom appear themselves as tutelary figures in her mature work). The young poet read H.D.'s war *Trilogy* as its volumes were published, and this confrontation of a woman poet with quotidian life and spiritual quest in wartime may have helped form her own lifetime concern, in her work, with the connections between public events, private life, and the broader and less predictable life of the mind. The presence of Joyce's ludic and radical derangement of language is also indubitable and warmly acknowledged. An early poem, "Private and Profane," names some of the other figures in her intellectual hagiography: Mary Wortley Montague, John Skelton, Mathias Grünewald, Mozart, Couperin, St. Thomas Aquinas, John Donne, Jane Austen. (I would add Montaigne and William Blake.) But the war years were also the time when her pacifist convictions were both tested and examined, and in which she found the resource of engagement with the pacifist *Catholic Worker* newspaper, co-founded by Dorothy Day.

In 1948, she went to Paris, where she pursued postgraduate studies at the Sorbonne and worked as an archivist for UNESCO.

It was on the boat to France that she made the acquaintance of another young poet, Lawrence Ferlinghetti, who would, eight years later, publish her first book. In Paris, she met the painter Claude Ponsot, whom she married in December 1948; their first child, Monique, was born there in September of the following year. The family then moved to New York, living first in Little Italy and then in Jamaica, Queens. Six more children, all boys, were born between 1951 and 1962.

Ponsot had been writing poems since her childhood, and, as *Springing*, her volume of new, selected, and uncollected poems shows, her mature style, with its modulations, its prosodic fine-tuning, its concentric ripples of context, was more than implicit in poems she wrote in her twenties. But she was (and still is) reticent about publication. It was the good taste of her fellow-ex-expatriate Lawrence Ferlinghetti, who, in San Francisco, had founded the City Lights Bookshop and its accompanying publishing venture, that brought her work into print. *True Minds*, solicited by Ferlinghetti, was published in 1956 in his Pocket Poets series, best known for (in the same year) the publication of Allen Ginsberg's *Howl*, but also of books by Denise Levertov and Frank O'Hara.

The serendipitous incongruity of Marie Ponsot's work first appearing in the context of the Beat explosion leads a reader to think of her in the context of her astounding generation of American poets, those born in the 1920s. Ginsberg, O'Hara, Levertov, Hayden Carruth, James Wright, Carolyn Kizer, Anthony Hecht, James Merrill, W. S. Merwin, Jane Cooper, John Ashbery are only some of them: the range of approaches, contexts, connections, ruptures, and evolutions in style seems infinite, as does their breadth of development, response, and reaction to what had become the modernist canon. While most of these poets were and are involved in schools, movements, circles of literary criticism and influence, Ponsot has made her own, initially fairly isolated way, though her prodigious and continual reading has connected her with all the possibilities—the choices of her contemporaries, the parallel development of pre- and post-war French writing, and of Irish writing—but also, perennially, English, French, and Latin poetry of the preceding centuries. The "argument" (particularly in the sense of "dialogue") and reconciliation of past and present are constant undercurrents in her poetry, whatever the primary theme.

In the years following the publication of *True Minds,* Marie Ponsot wrote much, published little of her own, but began a parallel career as a translator, ranging from classic fairy tales (her fascination with tales and fables transfigured what would have been mere bread-and-butter work for another writer) to verse drama by Paul Claudel for radio broadcast. There was a sequence of poems in *Poetry* duly acknowledged by a prize. There was a divorce. In 1965, Ponsot published her verse translations of a significant selection of La Fontaine's *Fables* with Signet Books. The project of a verse translation of the *Lais* of Marie de France did not survive the loss of the manuscript-in-progress. (The La Fontaine book was re-issued in 2002 by Welcome Rain Press.)

In 1966, as a single mother of seven, Marie Ponsot began what was to become a passionately committed teaching career, in the SEEK program at Queens College. She remained at Queens College for thirty years (eventually as a tenured full professor), and continues to teach in the graduate writing programs at New York University and Columbia University, as well as at the 92nd Street Y. Her teaching commitment began and has always been rooted in the teaching of composition (which in her mind is in no way different in kind from the teaching of "creative writing"). It led her to co-author with her colleague, scholar and writer Rosemary Deen, two invaluable and practical texts on the teaching of composition (useful for any writer, at any time): *Beat Not The Poor Desk* and *The Common Sense,* published by The Boynton Press in 1981 and 1985 respectively. In 1986, she spent a semester teaching in mainland China.

In 1981, Alfred A. Knopf published *Admit Impediment*—whose title wryly indicated its connection with and disjunction from the earlier volume. But while the first collection had been chapbook-brief, the new book, the work of a woman in the prime of life, was polyvalent and generous in its scope as well as in its length, in its formal, intellectual, and affective claims for the possibilities of poetry. *The Green Dark* was published in 1988, and *The Bird Catcher* in 1998: it received the National Book Critics' Circle Award, and an article by Dinitia Smith about the poet in

The New York Times signaled the beginning of an overdue critical acclaim. A new and selected poems, *Springing,* was published in the spring of 2002. It includes—as well as work completed since *The Bird Catcher*—previously unpublished or uncollected poems, many written between *True Minds* and the poems gathered in *Admit Impediment,* the work of a mature poet in her late thirties and forties, firm in her art but at that time apparently reticent about publication.

Ponsot is, despite the spacing of her book publications, a prolific poet, but she is a near-unbelievably exigent one, who will keep drafts of a significant work in progress for years, if necessary, until she is satisfied with it; who will even withdraw poems that have been published in journals from a book manuscript in progress for re-working she deems necessary. Apart from the demands of her life as a young, and then a single mother, it was this, and not any sparseness of the work itself, that resulted in the wide spacing of her first four published books.

Though Ponsot's work has not yet been extensively discussed in the context of second-wave American feminism, even by feminist critics, or made part of the feminist literary "canon," its assumptions, and, even more, the questions it poses, place it in that line (though never to the exclusion of other investigations). The poet considers the role of women in history, including the recovery of lost or insufficiently studied figures like Jacqueline Pascal (the poet-sister of Blaise, silenced in the Jansenist convent of Port-Royal) or Elena Cornaro (a seventeenth-century Italian, the first woman Doctor of Philosophy), but also the meaning of all women's exclusion from traditions of exploration and exchange. From her first book on, she observes and verbally constructs childbirth and mothering as essential human endeavors, not apart from but essential to the ongoing examined life and examined mind. A variety of ordinary women are given speech in her poems, often only discreetly indicated as dramatic monologues by the presence of quotation marks framing the text. Neither men nor women (nor children) are reified in her work: sexuality is appreciated, but divested of what she aptly names "the usual criminal metaphors."

Ponsot is a gardener and a birdwatcher, both of which are endeavors that imply a concentration of attention, a fine-tuning of observation, that are essential to her work as a poet. Poems such as "Gliding" (hang-gliders in the Alpes-Maritimes), "Pourriture Noble" (the creation of Sauternes), or "In Abeyance" (the migration of hawks above upstate New York) amaze the reader with the acuity of the poet's fine-tuned knowledge of *how and why something happens,* so that these events are never reduced to the facility of metaphor or simile, whatever other or larger human instance they may also imply. And it is because of (not "despite") the poet's polymath range of knowledge; because of the way she, teacher and mother, makes clear what she knows, that her work, while often complex and seldom predictable, remains not merely accessible but a source of joy and discovery to a wide range of readers.

While numerous reviewers have called attention to Ponsot's virtuoso performances in renewing received forms such as terza rima, the sonnet (and crown of sonnets), villanelle and sestina, rimas dissolutas and the Gaelic rann, not enough attention has been paid to her genius as a creator of nonce forms, in complex, sometimes long poems that visually resemble "free verse" but in which the reader aurally perceives patterns of meter, rhyme, and sonority which structure a complex progression of mental discovery. Even in elegies, her genius and penchant for wordplay are irrepressible—as if the human penchant for structuring words and syntax were, as it may well be, the mind's only bastion against death's annihilation. Death itself is disarmed in her poems by turns of phrase: "A decade, a week a second, then / time shrugs and shudders out of touch / into a perfect fit / and that's it" ("I've Been Around, It Gets Me Nowhere").

Marie Ponsot is at once a poet eminently of her time, whose work bridges the assimilation of and resistance to canonical modernism in contemporary Anglophone poetry, and one whose work is comprehensible as part of the ongoing enterprise of poetry as she understands it, not limited to national borders or to the English language, but an irreplaceable part of what defines the human mind and the human community.

Belfast Triptych

Medbh McGuckian's The Book of the Angel,
Seamus Heaney's District and Circle
and Derek Mahon's Harbour Lights

Here are important books by three major Northern Irish poets, poets who span that generation which will, I think, be remembered as marking an unprecedented flowering and fruition of poetry in Ireland. This generation also includes Eilean Ni Chuilleanan, Michael Longley, and Eavan Boland: it has witnessed (it has accomplished) the strenuous emergence of women poets in Ireland, "exceptions" no longer. Heaney, in fact, was McGuckian's teacher at Queen's College, Belfast, though only a dozen years separate them in age. While the books are different in conception and execution, each has as central to its construction one or two long poems or sequences, and each, from a point of view that seems individual, even private, re-establishes the role of the poet as witness to a place and time.

To a non-Irish reader, it often seems that the Irish poet inherits a vocation of representing Ireland even as s/he represents an individual whose speech earns its own keep, as well as "the poet" speaking from his or her vocation, out of and to a language itself. (For the Northern Irish poet to stand in for Ireland poses more complex problems.) The avatar of Heaney's Ireland is the isolated rural working man whose (masculine) artisan's craft is implicitly equated with the creation of poetry (as the avatar of Eavan Boland's is a suburban woman looking into the dusk from her doorway at a landscape scarred by history). Mahon here is the Irish writer as cross-cultural part-time expat, often looking homeward from a Joycean Paris, like his own Ulysses recalling

Ithaca on Calypso's isle. Medbh McGuckian tells us that her book's title comes from an Old Irish eighth-century document granting St Patrick ecclesiastical powers: a myth of spiritual and cultural origin.

There seems to be a marked dichotomy between male and female Irish poets of this generation on the question of metrical form. At least three notable male poets—Heaney, Mahon, and Paul Muldoon—are virtuosi of meter (and rhyme), a virtuosity which they deploy differently, but with similar bravura and obvious delight. Women poets whose careers span the same decades, whose backgrounds and formations are often congruent, Eilean Ni Chuilleanan, Eavan Boland, Paula Meehan, and Medbh McGuckian, have a more vexed relationship with metrics. (This resolved itself otherwise for poets born in the 1960s, such as Vona Groarke.) McGuckian has intense formal concerns, but they are entirely other than those of meter. Rather, hers is a prosody of displacement, unsettling the reader's expectations (just as meter might be said to satisfy them) with disjunctive imagery or phrasing enlivened by her lyricism.

Both McGuckian and Mahon center these recent books around what are to this reader fairly unpromising concepts: clouds for Mahon (who is at his best on terra firma); dreams and angels for McGuckian. Isn't this everything held most suspect in lyric poetry: cloud-cuckoo-land, the unwilled imagination, a mythology made suspect by overuse and fatuous belief. (Some survey said 70 percent of Americans interviewed "believe in angels." They believe American television commentators as well. Others may be warier.)

To state the obvious: McGuckian is a "difficult" poet, a difficulty which is made the more evident in juxtaposing her work with Heaney's and Mahon's. The latter especially is only too happy to spell out to his reader precisely what he's doing and what's going on: it's the meanders of his imagination and the connections he makes which are unpredictable, as well as his more savory rhymes. McGuckian, by contrast, makes connections by means of the shifting image: her shape-shifting syntax is not in the service of any easily perceptible narrativity or rhetorical structure, nor are her gifts of visual evocation used like Heaney's to create unequivocal, indelible tableaux. Noted for what has been called the "hypnotic oddness" of her verse, McGuckian owns up to the opacity of her work, acknowledging, "My words are traps / through which you pick your way" ("On Ballycastle Beach"). There is a kind of studied anti-intellectualism in some of McGuckian's interviews. Her work belies this, not because of its nonlinear or nonrepresentational character (which is also intensely intellectual) but because of the richness of reference, which informs it throughout, whether to the plastic arts, to Catholic hagiography, to history, or to literature. McGuckian's studied indirectness of approach might be compared with that of John Ashbery, in a different register, with more emphasis on sensory and sensual imagery. Her poetry connects the lyrical and the "experimental." There is a sense of corporeality in these poems, of embodiedness or incarnation, which provides grounding when sequential coherence is deliberately withdrawn.

> Ditch and pit and bridge and hearth
> and step and pool and kiln.
> The head on one bank, the body on the opposite,
> with the child asleep on the divine
> Easter of her breast.
>   ("In the Ploughzone")

Like it or not, then, here is a book returning obsessively to the idea of "angels" as messengers and observers, its title referring to St. Patrick's colloquy with one such (and thus an association with Ireland itself). In keeping with this theme, the untitled ten-poem Annunciation sequence is the book's central focus. It draws upon the perennial fertility (pun intended) of that myth and its hagiography, especially for women, women artists, in its celebration of inspiration, a sacred breath's incipient motion coming to a woman. What could be more like a Muse than Gabriel as he is habitually depicted? McGuckian does not give a referent for her apparently ekphrastic series of poems, which refer at times to paintings and at others to stained glass. Every reader attracted by this subject will have in her/his head at least a dozen such, Florentine, Flemish, French. I believe it is their juxtaposition we are invited to visualize as the backdrop, indeed as the foreground of these poems, where (as with the Flemish masters, who grounded sacred subjects in the quotidian), ex-centric details, in the corners, flying out of the field of vision, are equally significant, inform the import of the central figures' demeanor and movement:

> It is impossible to tell
> from the brocade and feathers
> of the robes, wings and hair of Gabriel,
> from the tartan cloth of the angel,
>
> whether he has already spoken.
> ("A Chrisom Child")

The poems are mostly stanzaic, in irregular quatrains or triplets, often enigmatically titled. "Chairé" suggests enthronement within a church; some may know that it's the Greek for "Ave." "A More" juxtaposes "amore" on "more" (the Shorter Oxford tells me that a "more" is also an obsolete word for a tree-stump) in a poem about Mary's confrontation with Gabriel "in a room neither can stand up in":

> The earth is spread out below them
> in small vanished areas of green vegetation,
> wood sorrel, the herb alleluia, an earlier meadow
> where they once stood fully upright.

Coming back obsessively to a moment before a momentous but internal action, the sequence is a series of unresolved confrontations, as the depictions of Annunciations partake of both motion and stasis. As at the moment the writer or painter puts pen or brush to paper or canvas, anything can happen, while, at the same time, a foretold story is embodying itself.

I don't know how much McGuckian wishes her reader to unravel the riddles she poses (the riddling woman is a staple of folk-tales) but there is some satisfaction when one does so. One of the most quietly powerful (and violent) of these poems is "Hand Reliquary, Ave Maria Lane," in which the scene that takes form after an elegiac opening is of a dying woman digging in her own palms with her nails to create stigmata. "A Lost Epistle to Sister Beatrice" *could* be in the voice of Dante:

> What if I never crush your ladyskin
> to open flight in a division of flesh,
> or place the eddies of a train
> hurled at the sea of your eyes?
> For whom, as for you, was the gate of heaven
> ever opened twice . . .

. . . though I'd be the last to assume that a poem of erotic longing written by a woman to a woman was in a male persona.

Derek Mahon is for me one of the most fraternal of poets, a nongendered quality he shares with Hayden Carruth, the nonrelated James Wright and Judith Wright, Carol Rumens and Louis MacNeice. His poetry engages the reader in colloquy. In the recent work especially, its conversational quality, its mimesis of the hesitations and forward thrusts of thought and informal speech, almost masks the poetry's craft and erudition.

MacNeice the Anglo-Irish cosmopolitan is an influence Mahon has himself cited. But it is Yeats with whom he dialogues most frequently in this book. There is a poem here entitled baldly "Lapis Lazuli" (dedicated to Harry Clifton, the same name if not the same man as Yeats's dedicatee). In Yeats's magnificent, problematic poem, it is "hysterical women" who, in 1938, foresee war, and quite specifically the Blitz. Cassandra is no more appreciated than she ever was—though one could say that Yeats with those lines incorporates the prophetic function while discrediting the women. And Edward Said could have had a field-day with Yeats's "Chinamen." (Yeats's message is that civilization will always be rebuilt by those who have retained joy in the face of disaster, but calling attention to the probable advent of disaster seems more sane than hysterical.) Mahon laconically defuses some of these problems while not-so-laconically claiming kinship and right of response. Formally, Yeats is the more "innovative" in his nonstanzaic alternations between tetrameter and pentameter: Mahon's poem is in dixains meandering between envelope quatrains separated by a couplet and alternating rhymes, all in the signature unbuttoned iambic pentameter of his recent work. (Mahon in the 1970s and 1980s favored tighter meter: this is a choice.) His lapis lazuli is a chunk in the rough, recalling the "whole night sky [as it] serves as a paperweight"— and, later in the poem, the post-war European continent glittering before the poet in his youth; the playful Chinese sages are the eponymous Deux Magots of the Paris café, not symbolic of a decorative Oriental wisdom but of the Haussmanian capital to which young Mahon escaped—and the "hysterical women" are replaced by:

> a young woman reads alone in a lighted train
> scratches her scalp and pushes specs in her hair,
> skipping the obvious for the rich and rare.
>
> Hope lies with her as it always does really . . .

Mahon's indirect colloquy with Yeats's continues more obliquely in "Cloud Ceiling"—also in dixains—for a child born to his late middle age, lowering the rhetorical level of "Prayer for My Daughter." Mahon's poem wishes the child nothing but a successful continuation of her infancy, acknowledging gladly that she won't be a heroine out of anyone else's myth; ruefully, that he "probably won't be here when you grow up". It is more of a meditation on the unknown realm from which the newly born emerge:

> An ocean-drop, dash in the dark, flash in the brain,
> Suspension in the red mist, in the light-grain,

than an imprecation or a prophecy. (The poem descends toward the occasional in its closing stanzas, after its bravura opening.)

While understanding why an Irish poet of sixty might feel obliged to "take on" Yeats, this reader would enjoy seeing Mahon "in dialogue" with MacNeice as well, if only because MacNeice's political-aesthetic model seems both more relevant to the present moment and more congenial to the persona and the aesthetic of Mahon's poetry; the formal largesse of some of his later poems is also in synch with Mahon's current impulse. But then this reader is one of the hysterical women.

Women, not hysterical, figure frequently in this book, not as the Other or even the Beloved, but as fellow humans: there is a three-sonnet sequence in the persona of Jean Rhys who could have been, and is not, caricatured as a Crazy Jane. The sequence is, instead, a portrait of a writer (*sa semblable, sa soeur*) surviving expatriation, poverty and drink, "fighting to keep sane / in a new age, and so the soul survives."

There is a double dialogue in *Harbour Lights*: with Yeats and Ireland; with France, French poets and Paris in particular, as if these two countries and literatures, the at-home and the abroad, were the double pole-star of Mahon's imagination (as has been evident throughout his career). The collection opens in Paris in wintertime, in a long poem called "Resistance Days," half of a diptych closing with the title poem, an equally lengthy internal monologue in Kinsale, County Cork. As well as Mahon's fluid version of Valéry's "Cimetière Marin," and his adaptation of Bonnefoy, the book includes a more subtle nod to Apollinaire in the poems "Shorelines" and "The Widow of Kinsale," an ekprastic poem and a dramatic monologue, both in five-line trimeter stanzas, closely resembling those of the "Chanson du Mal-Aimé" (used for a similar subject in *The Hunt by Night*). Juxtaposed versions of playful courtly love poems by Guillaume IX d'Aquitaine (twelfth century) and Tadgh O'Ruairc (seventeenth century), from the Occitan and the Irish respectively, emphasize these alternating currents in Mahon's work. These, as well as the Jean Rhys triptych and the above-mentioned "Widow," create a necessary counterpoint to the voice of the poet-persona and the associated pentameter dixains or octets which comprise much of the book.

But it is in the two long poems "Resistance Days" and "Harbour Lights" that Mahon, stepping free of influence and its anxieties, shows what he does best, allowing himself to be loquacious, even long-winded, in deceptively conversational verse. It is not the fact that the verse, when one examines it, is crafted, with every metrical expansion or rhyme furthering its project, which is remarkable, but that the poet does in these poems what novelists like Flaubert (and early Joyce) do: creates a character, his situation and history, his placement in the events of his time, with an accretion of seemingly local and domestic detail:

> The sort of snail-mail that can take a week
> but suits my method, pre-informatique,
> I write this from the St-Louis, rm. 14,
> —or type it, rather, on the old machine . . .
> ("Resistance Days")

> Alive to voices and, to my own surprise
> up with the lark, up with the June sunrise
> I study the visible lines of tidal flow,
> the spidery leaves alive with sweat and dew,
> doors blazing primary colours, blue and red,
> phone-lines at angles against bundling cloud.
> ("Harbour Lights")

What Mahon risks in this technique is loss of the lyric's memorability. But that does not seem to be his project or his aim. There are poems to which the reader returns because they have imprinted themselves on her consciousness, almost asking to be learned by heart; there are others, and Mahon's in this book are among them, to which one returns to resume a conversation.

Whereas Mahon's and McGuckian's poems, different as they are, suggest fluid motion in space and time, there is a solidity of place, and of objects, in the poetry of Seamus Heaney, with an emphasis on the perceived material thing, its implications suggested. As early as his signature poem "Digging," Heaney had equated the poet's pen with his father's spade; with a gun couched in his hand as well. The spade returns in "Poet to Blacksmith," what we are told is a translation of an eighteenth-century Irish poem by Eoghan Rua O' Súilleabháin, addressed to one Séamus McGearailt:

> Séamus, make me a tool to take on the earth,
> A suitable tool for digging or grubbing the ground,
> . . . .
> The plate and the edge of it not to be wrinkled or crooked—
> . . . .
> And the best thing of all, the ring of it, sweet as a bell.

The poem is in three rhymed alternating quatrains, lines of twelve to fourteen syllables, mostly in amphibrachs (I do not know if this echoes the Irish form). The combination of long lines and lilting, unfamiliar triple meter gives the poem an air of an anthem—all the more so as Heaney quotes from it in the last stanza of the poem which follows. With "Digging" in so many of Heaney's readers' minds, it resembles the insertion of a leitmotif, with a glint of self-mockery not present in the earnest early poem. Here the forging of the tool is the act of writing poetry itself, rather than the spade made equivalent to the pen. Other objects central to poems are "The Turnip-Snedder" (Heaney's genius for employing words at once homely and arcane is deployed from the opening poem onwards), a sledge-hammer, a saw, a fireman's helmet, a harrow-pin. Even a love poem, "Tate's Avenue," is limned in terms of three different car rugs spread on the ground by the couple over the years of their relationship. In the poem "To George Seferis in the Underworld" (one of a dozen homages to dead poets) Heaney retraces the process by which a local word from early life occurred to him and tells us, finally, what it means:

> And for me a chance to test the edge
> of seggans, dialect-blade
> hoar and harder and more hand-to-hand
> than what is common usage nowadays:
> sedge—marshmallow, rubber-dagger stuff.

Heaney is one of the contemporary masters of the sonnet in English, not surprising given his love of the well-defined, useful well-crafted object. There are numerous sonnets in *District and Circle*, including two sequences—the number depending on how one counts sonnet-like thirteen-liners. The sequences, the title poem and "The Tollund Man in Springtime," inform each other: one is a descent into the underworld (of the Underground) and the other an imagined resurrection. It is the alter ego Heaney created in *The Spirit Level* who is resuscitated into the contemporary world. (The Tollund Man lived during the fourth century BC. Executed or sacrificed, he was buried in a peat bog on the Jutland Peninsula in Denmark.) It is the Dantean poet who descends. The "District and Circle" poems contrast with the Olympian largesse of the Tollund sequence, all in

Petrarchan sonnets: here, the rhyme scheme is irregular, and three of the poems have only thirteen lines. The speaker, though he's got a ritual with a tin-whistle-playing busker, seems as alien to daily commuting as Dante (or the Tollund Man) would have been. His gestures are akin to those of remembered figures who "swing a sledge" or "forge a spade":

> Stepping on to it across the gap,
> On to the carriage metal, I reached to grab
> The stubby black roof-wort and take my stand
> From planted ball of heel to heel of hand

Despite their placement in the book, "District and Circle" seems to continue and complete the arc launched by "The Tollund Man" with the speaker once more underground, in perpetual purgatorial motion:

> And so by night and day to be transported
> Through galleried earth with them, the only relict
> Of all that I belonged to, hurtled forward . . .

—representing not only himself, but his "father's face in my own, waning / And craning." An old world set into motion in the new.

This is one of the few places in the book where there is vulnerability in the poet's stance, even though the world's uncertainty is often acknowledged. The Golden Age of his childhood was, as he depicts it, also a Bronze Age (thus his sense of kinship with the Tollund Man?) of "hoar and harder" words and wordless epiphanies. This is underscored by his returning here to themes, forms, and subjects he has considered before: the Tollund Man, his brother's death in childhood, old age and death in the country, homages to Wordsworth, Milosz, or Auden, conjugal eros with a welcome gleam of lust but a curiously absent Thou. The upper-middle-class complacency of the bloke in "The Birch Grove" as he "dandles a sandal" and watches his wife pouring tea seems to be tempting the gods. There were newly planted gardens in the suburbs of Nagasaki, Pompeii, and Beirut. *Carpe diem* by all means, but vouchsafe us a word to show you're aware of doing so. (Are the fourteen-/fifteen-syllable largely dactylic lines meant to remind us of Rome?) In the brief poem "Höfn," Heaney says beautifully enough that we've been told the glacier will melt and "come[s] wallowing across the delta flats." He observes it from an airplane and remarks (only) that its coldness still seems word-chillingly fearsome. A poet often enough doesn't know where the poem will go, but still, this reads like an evasion of its premise. I'm reminded of how in (again) "Lapis Lazuli," Yeats avoids confronting the prophecy of the opening stanza: London will be bombed. In both cases, the resulting poem is more interesting than any doom-saying, but the reader is still thinking "What about . . . ?" in the end.

Heaney's best poems resemble the objects, and the mostly stoic souls they describe and laud, in that they stand individual, discrete in the reader's memory: the country funeral of an aunt with "the hawthorn half in leaf" in terza rima in "The Lift"; the eroticism by indirection of "Tate's Avenue"; the three-part elegy for Milosz; the ominous "flicker-lit" title sequence.

These poets give us three lively, valid, and necessary possibilities for poetry: a riddling, arcane, and open-ended spell or charm; a colloquy with a reader imagined into dialogue; a concrete thing made of words and made to last.

Hédi Kaddour

Even in these days of electronic mail and mass transit, I suspect that the writer-flâneur still exists in every city. I know he, sometimes she, still strolls through and observes Paris, the city meant for walkers, where the idea of the ambulant urban spectator originated, in the works of Baudelaire, Walter Benjamin, Aragon—the "paysan de Paris"—Raymond Queneau, and Jacques Réda. One of his current incarnations is a slender man in jeans and a black leather jacket, pale, slightly unshaven, with a shock of wavy black hair, a wry smile, listening to an omnipresent Walkman or, these days, occasionally consulting a text on a SmartPhone. Many of Hédi Kaddour's poems arise from observations, from situations seized *sur le vif,* that might be ordinary but are nonetheless emblematic—of contemporary life, of human stubbornness, human invention or human cruelty, of the way the past invisibly inflects and inflicts the present.

I first encountered a group of Hédi Kaddour's poems in the summer of 2000, in *Po&sie,* the literary journal founded by the poet and philosopher Michel Deguy: a sequence of fourteen-liners with the general title "Passage au Luxembourg." They were a walker's, a watcher's, and a listener's poems, sonnet-shaped vignettes with a line or two of dialogue that turned the observation and the poem itself into a kind of miniature theater piece. I was, at the time, writing a sequence of flâneur sonnets myself, located across the river in another arrondissement, and the pleasurable exercise of translating these poems by a writer hitherto unknown to me (about whom the contributor's note told me little but that there were two books of his poems I might read) seemed like an extension of the work, or the walk, already in progress. It turned out that the poet and translator Claire Malroux, with whom I had worked in both directions, knew

Hédi Kaddour from the circle around the journal. I wrote to him, and in response, Claire and I were both invited to dinner—and a short piano recital by their music conservatory student daughter—by the poet and his wife on the Boulevard du Port-Royal. This was the beginning of a conversation—about poetry, politics, history, the novel, language, memory—that has gone on intermittently until today, over the time in which I did the translations in this book. Much of what I write here about the poet and his work is the fruit of such conversation.

Hédi Kaddour was born in Tunis, Tunisia in 1945 to a Tunisian father and a French Algerian pied-noir mother. He has lived in France since the age of eight, and French is his mother tongue. His view of poetry, though, is that of a comparatist—of a reader owing no allegiance to a single language or a single poetics: the poetries of several languages and literary traditions are lively and constant presences in his mind and in his work. He describes the occasion of writing his first poem: while a teacher of French in Morocco, in the dull stretch of time spent proctoring a long exam, he was reading a poem of Trakl's in a German/French bilingual edition. Dissatisfied with the translation, be began to re-translate parts of the text himself, then followed his own lines, rather than the German original, until he had, almost to his surprise, a poem of his own.

Some of the picaresque unpredictability in the life and point of view of this writer are contained in the anecdote. German is his second language, learned at school and pursued at university. Hölderlin, Heine, Rilke, and Trakl figure in his poetic pantheon alongside Baudelaire, Apollinaire, Supervielle, Mallarmé, and the contemporaries Jaccottet, Bonnefoy, Du Bouchet, Réda, and Deguy. Apollinaire himself knew German well. Kaddour notes that in the "Rhenanes," Apollinaire's deliberate insertion of "Germanisms" in syntax or idiom, directly translated into French, creates an atmosphere of alterity in these oblique narratives. He has occasionally adopted this technique of assimilated translation into his own work, often in less predictable contexts, steering a poem that begins anecdotally into the less certain and less known.

Kaddour did his French military service in Morocco, in part because of the possibility of joining (and eventually becoming the captain of) a fencing team. He used the opportunity to thoroughly master both literary and dialectal Arabic, and embark on the reading of that literature, finally adding an additional university degree in Arabic to those he already had in French literature. He stayed on in Morocco with his wife and daughters for a dozen years as a teacher of French. He has mentioned in conversation that part of his apprenticeship in Arabic consisted of listening to tapes made for him by friends of classical and contemporary poetry and fiction even before he could fully understand the texts. This oral reception of text and tongue remains important to him regardless of the language in question: recorded books in German or English (in which he is not yet completely fluent) often accompany him these days on his walks through the city.

Upon returning to France in the late 1980s, he worked as a journalist for the magazines *L'Autre Journal* and *Politis* for two years, and then continued writing music and theater criticism for the *Nouvelle revue française* while pursuing a teaching career at the École Normale Supérieure. He also undertook translations of contemporary German poets including Ingeborg Bachmann and Durs Grünbein, and has prefaced the work of Hans Magnus Enzensberger for the paperback classic Poésie Gallimard series. He began publishing his own poetry in the 1980s, first with small presses, Obsidiane and Ipomée, and later with Gallimard. He is also an expert in European classical music (the aforementioned daughter is now an emerging concert pianist), and a bemused/amused scholar and observer of modern and contemporary history, with a particular interest in the events surrounding and subsequent to World War I. After years in the fifth arrondissement, he presently lives in one of Paris's near suburbs—still an easy walk into the city center. He is a frequent contributor to the *Nouvelle revue française* and a member of the editorial committee of *Po&sie*. Kaddour's journalist's skills and instinct, for observation, for seizure of the salient detail, are put to work in his poems, as is the invaluable ability to become a "significant absence"—not a Rimbaldian absconder but an observer who eschews inference—from many of his own texts. He also cites the theater critic's skill of capturing in a few concise sentences something of the narrative, the direction, the physical presence, the actors' interpretation of a play as something that has served, indeed helped to shape his own goals as a poet. The dramatist and the reporter are both at work in many poems here, as in the opening of "The Question":

> Do you work for the dough or to
> Get laid, *the nurse is asked by*
> *A woman who's brought in by the police*

Kaddour's work combines an often surprising sensuality with erudition and wit, while it questions the structures of syntax itself, and the limits of poetic form. He, along with his friend and contemporary Guy Goffette, is one of the few current French poets whose work one could place in a direct line from that of Jacques Réda and Jacques Roubaud—but where the horizons of Réda's poems tend to be local, Kaddour's vary. There is a strain of his poetic work that is as local and specific to his urban residence as are the Paris poems of Baudelaire, Apollinaire, Prévert or Queneau. An observed singular occurrence, a coincidence, a situation at once natural and unexpected, will be the starting point of one of his compressed narratives:

> What has gotten into the bus driver
> Who has left his bus, who has sat down
> On a curb on the Place de l'Opéra
> ("The Bus Driver")

Walking along the river, purchasing a pastry in a bakery, a few words exchanged with a bookseller, waiting in line at a concert hall, may provide Kaddour with the start of a poem: notes taken on the spot, never a solitary meditation over a blank piece of paper. Other poems, however, have the breadth, even in condensed forms, of the work of Walcott or MacNeice. These sometimes focus on the intersections of French and North African history, sometimes on the tortuous evolution of Europe after World War I:

> But Arabs, you know
> what hotheads they are . . . Her husband shut her up, left
> first

> came back plus a medal, less a leg, a list
> of all the Mohammeds dead at Verdun. She exclaimed "It's
> madness, not you, there in Russia . . ."
>
> ("Poppies")

Many poems evoke other poets whose work is a continual reference point for the writer, with a technique not dissimilar to Guy Goffette's *Dilectures,* engaging at once with the other's text and persona. A phrase, an image or an anecdote gives rise to a concise portrait, a dialogue with more than a homage to Borges, Celan, Brodsky, the politically engaged Czech poet Vladimir Holan, the French minimalist Jean Follain, the trilingual Alsatian Jean-Paul de Dadelsen.

> *. . . he's put* white tulips
> *Instead of* black firs: *Paul*
> *Celan didn't like tall trees. You*
> *Never knew him, and you like these poems?*

—a bookseller asks the narrator in "Quai des Orfèvres."

As these names imply, Kaddour's references range from the undisputed figures of "world" poetry, translated into every language, to somewhat marginalized, non-mainstreamed (and rarely translated) French ones.

Still, most of the poetic encounters that Kaddour describes as crucial to his own formation as a writer are with European writers of other-than-French language and history, and often with the experience of displacement or exile. One of his signal discoveries was Joseph Brodsky's essay collection *Far from Byzantium* in the late 1980s (in Laurence Dyère and Veronique Schilz's French translation), which he read along with Brodsky's poetry: essays which are meditations on history as well as on the work of individual poets: Akhmatova, Mandelstam, Tsvetaeva, but also Cavafy, Auden, and Walcott. His presentation of Brodsky in an essay of his own in the *NRF* in 1989 constituted the serious introduction of the Russian émigré poet to a French readership. Kaddour found in Brodsky something of a kindred spirit: a writer who had endured history's horrors and vagaries, but (or therefore) remained skeptical and independent of political and aesthetic pieties, steeped in the classical traditions of his own

and other literatures while open to an absolute contemporaneity. From "A Victim's Soul," Kaddour's poem-homage to Brodsky:

> But one day he emptied his closets
> Of suits which would have been all too
> Becoming to the enemy, and he went off
> Towards a wind from beyond those lands.

Literature, for Hédi Kaddour, whether it be poetry or fiction, is
also the past of literature—the poetry of today contains the poetry
of the past. Writing cannot be all memory, or it would satisfy itself
with repeating the past, which would produce, at best, mass-
market literature; but neither can it eliminate memory totally: in
that case, it condemns itself to be disposed of in its turn. That, he
says is the meaning of Jules Supervielle's reference to "oublieuse
mémoire"—*forgetful memory*, forgetfulness in order not to repeat
what was previously done; memory so as not to succumb to am-
nesia. Kaddour shares with Brodsky too an obliquity of approach:
the life of the polis is present in his poems, injustice and violence
as well, but seen from an angle, and never editorialized upon.

Kaddour's poetry often dialogues with classical forms, with
the sonnet in particular—though he uses the fourteen-line
poem in a way that might remind American readers of Robert
Lowell's quatorzains, especially of the volume called *History*, in
its collaging of public and private events, and its urban portraits.
Kaddour's collection *Passage au Luxembourg* is, except for one
poem, made up entirely of a hundred-odd quatorzains. It contains a sequence congruent with the title, another based on
scenes from Breughel, which are more portraits of carnal
human nature than ekphrastic poems. Other poems achieve (as
sonnets can) a delicate and witty balance between eroticism and
a certain misanthropy, which is not at all misogyny. Even the
erotic poems maintain a delicate balance in locating the
speaker: either a narrator or a participant in the act might describe the woman in "High Cheekbones":

> . . . . She was the first
> To kiss and is still surprising herself
> With her own sweetness as she watches her leg
> Rise towards the antique chandelier.

Kaddour has played with the formal aspect in successive versions of these poems, initially using the classical structure of two quatrains and two tercets, then closing up the poems into a single bloc, sometimes drastically shortening the lines. In English we are more used to identifying as "sonnets" poems which are not broken into four quatrains and two tercets. French poetic nomenclature has resisted this, leading in part to a paucity of discussion of the contemporary French sonnet, a near-assumption of its demise, while a foreign reader would see its continuation, in Roubaud, certainly, but also in Kaddour and Goffette.

Hédi Kaddour makes a surprisingly sharp differentiation between his own urban "sonnets" and Baudelaire's. In Baudelaire, and I would add, in Verlaine, and in the work of Guy Goffette as well, a subjectivity inherited from the Romantics is almost persistently present, whereas in Kaddour's poems, it is more frequently absent except in the persona of a bemused and not at all omniscient observer: a trait shared with Apollinaire's "Rhénanes," or the short poems of Jean Follain (these latter resemblances pointed out by Kaddour himself). The absent "I" is not uncommon in contemporary French poetry, but the insistent lively presence of a quotidian specific not overshadowed by subjectivity sets Hédi Kaddour's poetry somewhat apart. If he resembles the Lowell of *History*, the "confessional" aspect of *The Dolphin* is entirely foreign to his project—while the narrative arc fragmented into salient anecdote in independent poems which could also be viewed as stanzaic, found in (for example) Hayden Carruth or in contemporaries like George Szirtes, Alfred Corn, or Derek Mahon, is more familiar to it. These correspondences are my own interjections. Kaddour's frame of reference in contemporary poetry is not predominantly Anglophone—his touchstones in American poetry are William Carlos Williams and Wallace Stevens—unless the exiled Brodsky can also be considered an American poet.

The poems in this collection are taken from three books published by Gallimard: *La fin des vendanges* (1989); *Jamais une ombre simple* (1994); and *Passage au Luxembourg* (2000). Following the poet's arrangement of his own books, I have taken the liberty of arranging them more thematically than chronologically: poems to do with history and with precursors; poems that cross Paris on foot; poems to do with erotic and familial relations—and with music, which is always close to the intimate for this poet. Hédi Kaddour's first novel, *Waltenberg*, was published by Gallimard in 2005 and received the Prix Goncourt du premier roman: an English translation has been published in Great Britain. (One day, he says, he came home from a stroll in the city with notes for a poem; developing them, he realized that he was going to write a long novel instead—though some of the themes of the novel had already been addressed in a play written in the 1990s.) He is at present completing a second novel, in tandem with a nonfiction prose narrative that combines acute informal literary criticism with the kind of witty, honed fine observation of quotidian life in Paris I find in his poems (both to be published in 2010 by Gallimard). And first drafts of their chapters were also composed while walking across the pont d'Austerlitz from the Thirteenth Arrondissement to the quai de la Rapée or alongside the sailboat pond in the Luxembourg Gardens on a foggy October afternoon.

Three American Women Poets in the First Century of World Wars

> American poetry has been part of a culture in conflict.
> . . . We are a people tending toward democracy at the
> level of hope; at another level, the economy of the
> nation, the empire of business within the republic,
> both include in their basic premise the idea of
> perpetual warfare.
> —Muriel Rukeyser, *The Life of Poetry* (1949)

> The impulse to enter, with other humans, through
> language, into the order and disorder of the world, is
> poetic at its root as surely as it is political at its root.
> —Adrienne Rich, *What Is Found There* (2002)

Muriel Rukeyser began an untitled poem of the 1960s: "I lived in the first century of world wars." I suspect many people now fear that we live in the second. Sometimes a column by an astute political journalist seems more necessary than poetry, and effaces the desire for it. Still, it is not the journalism of the past which, at the bleakest or most hopeful moments, calls for rereading. I return to the poetry of Akhmatova, Paul Celan, Adrienne Rich, or Mahmoud Darwish, poets variously engaged in and part of the largest human world, because their writing convinces me that poetry remains necessary, intrinsic to more than one kind of understanding.

I think of this in the context of the work of three poets, American women, confronted with seismic change, moral and physical danger, injustice and with a consequent devaluation of the poet's work, even as that work seems, to the writer, most urgent. All three responded, not with lyric exclamation or dithyrambic indictment, but with long, complex poems in discrete sections which inscribe themselves in the epic tradition: book-length poems narrating the destiny of a people, recognizing the significance of contemporary events in relation to the past.

H.D., christened Hilda Doolittle in Bethlehem, Pennsylvania, in 1886, lived as an expatriate in England and Switzerland after 1911. She had many reasons to engage with an epic tradition: the most obvious, lifelong, largely autodidactic commitment to classical and pre-classical Greek poetry and drama. Poems written in the 1920s and 1930s utilize self-translated fragments from Sappho, and lines by obscure poets, often women, in the Greek Anthology, upon which she constructed narratives and dramatic monologues. But the poem I would call epic, the *Trilogy* composed in London in 1942–1944 is more complex in its collage of past and present, in its attempted synthesis of diverse myths and bodies of knowledge, and particularly in its simultaneous confrontation with contemporaneity and interiority. Might that be a characteristic of the "woman's epic"—a recognition of the seamlessness of the private and the public life, of how "the personal is political," as the women's movement put it, and how the political is also personal?

H.D.'s friend, patron, sometime lover, and forty years' companion Winifred Bryher wrote adventure novels and memoirs, not poetry; her own life had epic (and adventurous) resonance. When World War II broke out in Europe, Bryher was doing rescue work with the Red Cross in neutral Switzerland. H.D. was in London. Bryher tried to persuade H.D., who had been traumatized by the first war in London, to join her. H.D. refused. So Bryher, in September of 1940, made a difficult journey into the besieged city, and stayed with H.D. in London for the remainder of the war, organizing the practical side of their lives.

Trilogy breaks with H.D.'s early work, and with the restrictive label of "Imagist." Alongside her modernist colleagues Pound, Eliot, and Williams, she composed a poem encompassing the major themes of twentieth-century poetry: world war, experienced at first-hand by civilians as well as soldiers; the recovery of an idea of self and society in social fragmentation; the confusion and liberation arising from changing gender relations; the desire to synthesize plural religious and mythic traditions into a plausible faith; a redefinition of the nature and uses of the arts and the imagination.

Each of the three books has its own focus. *The Walls Do Not Fall* moves cinematically from views of London during the Blitz with houses cut open like dioramas in a museum, to intense close-ups of humble creatures, the mollusc enclosed in its shell creating a "pearl of great price," the despised worm revealed as a caterpillar which will "weave its own shroud" and emerge transformed. Iconic images of Egyptian rulers and deities, and their relation to Judeo-Christian and Hellenic tradition, inform the poems of *Trilogy*, in counterpoint to the destruction visited on London by the German bombing, enriching and complicating a narrative palimpsest. In *Tribute to the Angels,* a series of hieratic portraits of angelic figures culminates in a persistent dream-vision of a Lady who corresponds to many and yet to none of the images of saints, the Virgin or pagan goddesses, bearing a blank book which will contain "the still-unwritten pages of the new." *The Flowering of the Rod* tells an apocryphal tale embroidering on Scripture in which Kaspar, one of the Magi (associated by the poet with Freud—whose analysand and student H.D. had been in 1933–34) is inspired to a vision of universal order by an encounter with Mary Magdelene, herself identified with pre-Adamic goddesses.

Formally, each of the three long poems consists of forty-three individual numbered lyrics, most no longer than a page. All but one are in short-lined couplets. Each is a single sentence composed of multiple linked segments: full stops occur only at the end of individual numbered poems. In this unity, *Trilogy* resembles pre-modernist epics, which rely on continuous form, and differs from poems of its own era like the *Cantos* or *The Waste Land,* notable for deliberate irregularity. It is also unlike H.D.'s earlier lyrics, whose stanzas are typically of uneven length and unpredictable shape. There is a consistent weaving of the contemporary and the mythical, of Christian and pagan images. The ruins of bombed London are viewed on a palimpsest of the ruins of Pompeii and Egypt. The discredited writer is reinstated as "the scribe." Multiple mythologies of female gods and icons are resurrected, not to overthrow but to interact with and enrich the masculine panoply. In contrast to the "verse paragraph" of poetic authority, H.D.'s couplet/paragraphs in *Trilogy* include more space, more silence around the words, elicit, often explicitly, a response from the reader. The work is much more concerned with internal struggle than the traditional epic; yet it aspires to represent, not an individual's experiences, but a generation's. *Trilogy* opens a plural dialogue—with Freud, with Bryher, with the reader—in quest of some wisdom at work in the world during "the days of Mars"—as Bryher was to entitle her own war memoir.

H.D. was one of a generation of American expatriates: Pound, Gertrude Stein, Eliot, Djuna Barnes. In contrast, most of the American poets born just before and during World War I did most of their work within the borders of the United States, however much they traveled (Elizabeth Bishop, from her Canadian childhood on, was an exception). Gwendolyn Brooks, though born in Kansas in 1917, lived in Chicago through the eight decades of her life. If the purpose of the epic is "to give meaning to the destiny of a people, recognizing the significance of contemporary events in relation to the past," one might say that all of Brooks's work had epic intentions; Its focus was always, above all, a community, her own African American community in Chicago. Her first book, *A Street in Bronzeville,* published in 1945, when she was twenty-seven, vividly portrayed the lives of working-class black women and men coping with poverty and racism—sometimes with gallantry and wit; sometimes succumbing to the pressures. It also dealt with the effects of World War II on Brooks's neighbors. "Negro Hero" is based on an incident in the Pacific theater where a seaman, forbidden, because of his race, to bear arms, nonetheless picked up a machine gun and saved the lives of his fellow crewmen. "Gay Chaps at the Bar" provides an understated view (in sonnet-monologues) of the war's effect on young black enlisted men and officers.

Brooks's second book, *Annie Allen,* was published in 1949. Its focus is clearly on African American women. One narrative in discrete parts, it is the bildungsroman of a fairly sheltered lower-middle-class dark-skinned teenage girl, given to romantic fantasies. Like *Trilogy,* this is a narrative where the poet/narrator is largely absent except as an observer. But this narrative has a protagonist, who changes as a result of experience. The longest, central section of the poem depicts, at an ironic distance, her love affair and marriage with a man idealized beyond his possibilities. He departs as a soldier for World War II (which, given the date of the poem, did not have to be named). He returns, but not to Annie; to a more flamboyant woman with lighter skin. He comes back to Annie when he is dying, of a war-related disease, probably tuberculosis, leaving her a widow at "tweaked and twenty-four." This section's title, "The Anniad," recalls *The Iliad* or *The Aeneid,* implicitly comparing their subjects: heroes who go to war; women who stay at home and wait for them. It is written in seven-line rhymed stanzas of trochaic trimeter, in elaborate polysyllables. This is an obvious contrast with the expansiveness of an "epic" line: hexameters, the alexandrine, or iambic pentameter, which Brooks had and would use magisterially. It also recalls, in a different linguistic mode, H.D.'s short, "open" lines in *Trilogy.* But Brooks's language creates a distance between narrator and narrative, between the "knowing" speaker (and readers) and the naïve protagonist and her story. Still, it also invests the story with a kind of heraldic dignity, as well as a distinctly modernist distortion and exaggeration of quotidian events. One poem of which this section of *Annie Allen* is, to me, reminiscent, is Pope's *The Rape of the Lock*—in which a young socialite's dressing-table rites are described, in rhymed couplets, analogous to a knight's preparations for battle, and exaggeration leads to a diction prefiguring the surreal: a mock-epic. The events chronicled in "The Anniad" are not trivial: the sexual passion and union are, in the poem's world, real, the betrayal is real, and the shadowed death is real as well. But Brooks's choice of a tightly metered and pyrotechnically rhymed form in constant tension with her verbal exuberance adds both irony and constant musical tension to the poem.

There is, though, a striking contrast between "The Anniad" and the parts of *Annie Allen* preceding and following it, chronicling, respectively, Annie's childhood—in a neighborhood that's clearly in Gwendolyn Brooks's Chicago—and her life after the war. Like the poems of *A Street in Bronzeville,* these are "neighborhood" portraits: the meditations of a single woman raising a child, a plea for dignity in the eyes of her own community, her wavering faith in a post-war America whose new prosperity was not always shared by African Americans. But there is also a restaurant frequented by working-class blacks after a hard day, a drive into the suburbs, a funeral parlor that can't contain the life-force of a frequenter of bars, jazz-clubs, and Chicago streets. The book's progression and this last section's title, "The Womanhood," key the reader to the fact that these poems share the same protagonist. The young woman who *was* observed (by a skeptical if not cynical narrator) in "The Anniad" has been transformed into an acute observer of the world around her; the girl who lived in "romantic thralldom" has entered the larger world. The poet abandons the baroque diction of "The Anniad" for quotidian speech, and more expansive, less pyrotechnical metrics. The ironic narrator has been replaced by a speaker of transparent complexity, implicated in the life surrounding her.

Annie Allen was awarded the Pulitzer Prize in 1950—the first book by an African American poet to be so honored. Wallace Stevens was said to have remarked when the thirty-three-year-old Brooks arrived at the banquet, "Who let the coon in?"

Though one might speculate about how much the impact of World War II on these poets' lives moved them towards the broad canvas of the epic or mock-epic poem, both H.D. and Gwendolyn Brooks had an enduring interest in expanded form that continued after the war. H.D's next major work was *Helen in Egypt,* whose premise is an apocryphal Greek myth in which the actual Helen, replaced by a double, spent the Trojan War years in Egypt. Gwendolyn Brooks's 1963 multi-vocal narrative, "In the Mecca," is set within the confines of a huge decaying apartment building in Chicago, during the search for a missing child. This enclosure is a distinctly more dystopic vision of "community" than the streets, back yards, churches and bars of "Bronzeville."

I wonder if Gwendolyn Brooks in Chicago, where she steeped herself in the work of white American modernists along with the Harlem Renaissance poets, read *Trilogy* when it appeared during the war, or if H.D., in Switzerland, was sent the black poet's Pulitzer Prize–winning book in 1950. It is probable that Brooks had read the work of another poet with both epic and populist aspirations: her contemporary, Muriel Rukeyser.

Rukeyser's project as a poet was as inclusive as H.D.'s was sometimes hermetic, and her communities of choice were numerous.

From her first book, published in the Yale Younger Poets series when she was twenty-one, she showed her desire to examine and widen her own implications in the contemporary world through poetry. For her, poetry could encompass both science and history, that of the past and of the present, from the Depression through the anti-war movements in which the poet was active at the end of her career.

It was in the magazine *New Masses* in 1936 that she first read about Gauley Bridge, West Virginia, where numerous miners hired to dig tunnels in the mountains were falling ill and quickly dying of silicosis. There was considerable evidence that the mine owners knew of the danger, but instead of providing adequate protection, had widened the scope of the mining operation. The twenty-two-year-old Rukeyser drove to West Virginia with a woman photographer friend. She conducted and collected interviews with miners, white and black, with their wives, widows, and children, with mine employees. She collected documentary evidence—court transcripts and testimony, stock market reports, medical diagnoses. From this, Rukeyser constructed the multisectioned, multivocal *The Book of the Dead,* published in 1938. Here, an American poet attempts to deconstruct the contradictions of power and social justice, integrating implicating documents, scientific evidence, and the voices of ordinary people. The poet incorporates the documentary filmmaker's techniques. The eclipsed "I" of *The Book of the Dead* is more like a camera's eye than a poet-protagonist's.

As with Brooks's Bronzeville, the community of Gauley Bridge is itself the protagonist. The citizens' committee spearheading the investigation, made up of black and white miners and miners' widows, has both a choral and heroic role. Like Brooks as well, Rukeyser uses formal variety to individualize the voices and histories making up her mosaic: blank verse quatrains, modified terza rima, the blues stanza, eruptions of prose. The progression of fact and lyric, metered stanzas, dramatic monologue, pastoral, seemingly unadulterated prose testimony, usually in dialogue form, creates a sequence operatic in its registers and in its arias. In her finale Rukeyser connects the local present with a panoramic view of the continent, the histories working beyond and behind it: the reference to the Egyptian *Book of the Dead* in the title was not incidental. The poem's subject—Union Carbide's ruthless mining practices at the Gauley Bridge hydroelectric project in West Virginia—had captured national attention. Rukeyser's experiment raised questions of poetics, documentary conventions, modernist representation, and poetry's audience. It is possible that James Agee and Walker Evans's 1941 book of reportorial/poetic prose and photographs *Let Us Now Praise Famous Men* was influenced by Rukeyser's synthesis of lyric and documentary; her use of documents prefigures Williams's *Paterson* and Charles Reznikoff's *Testimony*.

Rukeyser, like Brooks and H.D., was to write work of ambitious scope throughout a life which epitomized the poet as witness. She was in Spain as a journalist at the outbreak of the Spanish Civil War. Thirty-five years later, she was arrested protesting the war in Vietnam. One of Rukeyser's last projects before her death in 1980 was "The Gates," a long poem written in South Korea where, representing American PEN, she protested the imprisonment of poet Kim Chi Ha. During the McCarthy years, the FBI kept a voluminous file on her. Her literary reputation, launched with prizes and acclaim in the 1930s, waned in the 1950s, victim of Red-baiting and a conservative or willfully apolitical "New Criticism." Although there is a resemblance between Ginsberg's Whitmanian line and inclusive, lamenting outsider's voice in "Howl" and much of Rukeyser's project—and they were both New York leftist Jews—her work was not a reference, or not cited by the Beat poets as such, during that movement's prominence in the 1960s.

These three American poets, the Pennsylvania expatriate, the working-class black Chicagoan, the leftist-activist New York Jew, demonstrate radical and radically different strategies with which poetry can confront and represent extreme situations. Each of their careers also demonstrates the danger of erasure that faces dissenting and unfashionable poetic voices, women's voices in particular, though by no means exclusively.

H.D. is the only one of these poets whose work is known outside the United States, not surprisingly, as she spent much of her life, and two world wars, in London. Still, she was for years anthologized and represented only by the Imagist poems of her youth, whose techniques inform her later work, but give no idea of its scope.

Brooks became an icon of the American Black Arts movement in the 1960s. As such she was expected to re-model her preoccupations and her prosody, to "unlearn technique," suppress irony, and—though it was never thus stated—to shift her focus from ordinary working-class black women and men to young male race revolutionaries. Her principled decision to publish only with small black-owned presses after 1968 had the unfortunate effect of making books written after that date difficult to obtain.

Rukeyser's 600-page *Collected Poems* was published in 1979, a year before her death: it went out of print soon afterwards. For more than a decade her work was unavailable, except in anthologies coming from the American feminist movement. Feminism was one of Rukeyser's causes, but neither the sole nor the primary one.

Today, the works of H.D., Rukeyser, and Brooks are the focus of important critical study, and can be read in new or reprint editions. Without the rescue effort made by American feminist editors and anthologists, and by African American editors and anthologists, these poets' work might have remained in the limbo of out-of-print books: a response to those who deplore "focused" anthologies as segregationist and reductive of those included.

The poet is at once essentially of her time, place, culture, language, and yet must be enough apart from them to make them comprehensible to someone whose placement is different. These poets' work, I believe, becomes comprehensible through its very specificity, while demonstrating innovative ways in which poetry responds to extreme situations. Specific though they are, the thematic and formal expansiveness of these books, their varied multivocal or exploded approach, inscribes them all in a line of modernism that redefines the long poem, the poem which reclaims the ground of narrative, social observation, character depiction, developed thought, from fiction and cinema, with a scope that could be called epic. While one can never be sure what reading has informed a poet's work, I can imagine that more recent long poem sequences like Suzanne Gardinier's *The New World,* Sharon Doubiago's *South America Mi Hija,* Marilyn Nelson's *The Homeplace,* Rachel Blau DuPlessis's *Drafts* were permitted some of their energy and invention by the books of H.D., Brooks, and Rukeyser.

UNDER DISCUSSION
Annie Finch and Marilyn Hacker, General Editors
Donald Hall, Founding Editor

Volumes in the Under Discussion series collect reviews and essays about individual poets. The series is concerned with contemporary American and English poets about whom the consensus has not yet been formed and the final vote has not been taken. Titles in the series include: